Rick Steves

POCKET

ROME

Rick Steves & Gene Openshaw

Contents

Introduction 3

Colosseum Tour 13

Roman Forum Tour 27

Heart of Rome Walk 43

Vatican Museums Tour 53

St. Peter's Basilica Tour 81

Borghese Gallery Tour 105

Sights 121

Sleeping 161

Eating 169

Practicalities.......................................183

Index 203

Introduction

Rome is magnificent and brutal at the same time. It's a showcase of Western civilization, with astonishingly ancient sights and a modern vibrancy. But with the wrong attitude, you'll be frustrated by the kind of chaos that only an Italian can understand. On my last visit, a cabbie struggling with the traffic said, *"Roma chaos."* I responded, *"Bella chaos."* He agreed.

Over two thousand years ago the word "Rome" meant civilization itself. Everything was either civilized (part of the Roman world) or barbarian. Today, Rome is Italy's political capital, the heart of Catholicism, and the center of its ancient empire, littered with evocative remains. As you peel through the city's fascinating layers, you'll find Rome's monuments, cats, laundry, cafés, churches, fountains, traffic, and 2.7 million people endlessly entertaining.

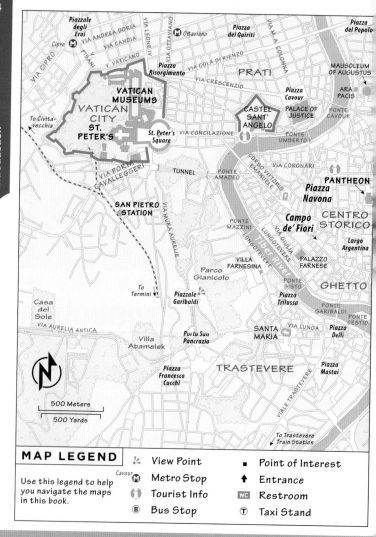

MAP LEGEND

Use this legend to help you navigate the maps in this book.

- ⅍ View Point
- Ⓜ Metro Stop
- 🛈 Tourist Info
- Ⓑ Bus Stop
- ▪ Point of Interest
- ♠ Entrance
- WC Restroom
- Ⓣ Taxi Stand

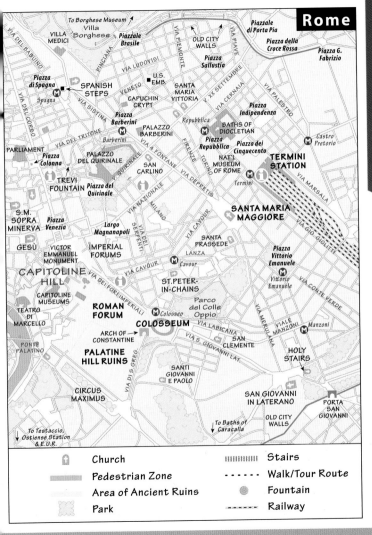

Rome

- VIA DEL BABUINO
- To Borghese Museum
- VILLA MEDICI
- Villa Borghese
- Piazzale Brasile
- PINCIANA
- VIA PIEMONTE
- OLD CITY WALLS
- VIA PLAVE
- Piazzale di Porta Pia
- Piazza della Croce Rossa
- VIA DI PORTA PIA
- Piazza G. Fabrizio
- VIA LUDOVISI
- Piazza Sallustia
- Piazza di Spagna
- SPANISH STEPS
- Spagna
- VENETO
- U.S. EMB.
- SANTA MARIA VITTORIA
- V. XX SETTEMBRE
- VIA CERNAIA
- VIA PALESTRO
- VIA DEL CORSO
- VIA SISTINA
- CAPUCHIN CRYPT
- Piazza Barberini
- PALAZZO BARBERINI
- Barberini
- Repubblica
- BATHS OF DIOCLETIAN
- Piazza Indipendenza
- Piazza dei Cinquecento
- Castro Pretorio
- PARLIAMENT
- VIA DEL TRITONE
- VIA 4 FONTANE
- FIRENZE
- Piazza Repubblica
- NAT'L MUSEUM OF ROME
- TERMINI STATION
- Piazza Colonna
- PALAZZO DEL QUIRINALE
- SAN CARLINO
- VIA DEPRETIS
- Termini
- VIA MARSALA
- TREVI FOUNTAIN
- Piazza del Quirinale
- TORINO
- VIA NAZIONALE
- MILANO
- SANTA MARIA MAGGIORE
- VIA GIO. GIOLITTI
- S.M. SOPRA MINERVA
- Piazza Venezia
- Largo Magnanapoli
- VIA DEL SERPENTI
- VIA CAVOUR
- SANTA PRASSEDE
- Piazza Vittorio Emanuele
- GESÙ
- VICTOR EMMANUEL MONUMENT
- IMPERIAL FORUMS
- VIA DEI FORI IMPERIALI
- LANZA
- Cavour
- Vittorio Emanuele
- VIA CONTE VERDE
- CAPITOLINE HILL
- ST. PETER-IN-CHAINS
- Parco del Colle Oppio
- CAPITOLINE MUSEUMS
- ROMAN FORUM
- Colosseo
- COLOSSEUM
- VIA LABICANA
- SAN CLEMENTE
- VIALE MANZONI
- Manzoni
- TEATRO DI MARCELLO
- PONTE PALATINO
- ARCH OF CONSTANTINE
- PALATINE HILL RUINS
- VIA S. GIOVANNI LAT.
- HOLY STAIRS
- VIA DI S. GREG.
- SANTI GIOVANNI E PAOLO
- VIA MERULANA
- CIRCUS MAXIMUS
- SAN GIOVANNI IN LATERANO
- PORTA SAN GIOVANNI
- OLD CITY WALLS
- To Testaccio, Ostiense Station & E.U.R.
- To Baths of Caracalla

Symbol	Meaning	Symbol	Meaning
	Church		Stairs
	Pedestrian Zone		Walk/Tour Route
	Area of Ancient Ruins		Fountain
	Park		Railway

About This Book

With this book, I've selected only the best of Rome—admittedly a tough call. The core of the book is six self-guided tours that zero in on Rome's greatest sights and neighborhoods. Do the "Caesar shuffle" through ancient Rome's Colosseum and Forum. Stroll from Campo de' Fiori to the Spanish Steps, lacing together Rome's Baroque and bubbly nightspots. Visit St. Peter's, the greatest church on earth, and learn something about eternity by touring the huge Vatican Museums. Savor the sumptuous Borghese Gallery.

The rest of the book is a traveler's tool kit. You'll find plenty more about Rome's attractions, from shopping to nightlife to less touristy sights. And there are helpful hints on saving money, avoiding crowds, getting around Rome, finding a great meal, and much more.

If you'd like more information than this Pocket Guide offers, I've sprinkled the book liberally with Web references. For general travel tips—as well as updates for this book—see ricksteves.com.

Rome—A City of Neighborhoods

Sprawling Rome actually feels manageable once you get to know it.

The historic core, with most of the tourist sights, sits inside a diamond formed by Termini train station (in the east), Vatican City (west), Villa Borghese Gardens (north), and the Colosseum (south). The Tiber River snakes through the diamond from north to south. At the center of the diamond is Piazza Venezia, a busy square and traffic hub. It takes about an hour to walk from Termini train station to Vatican City.

Think of Rome as a collection of neighborhoods, huddling around major landmarks.

Ancient Rome: In ancient times, this was home for the grandest

Rome's Neighborhoods

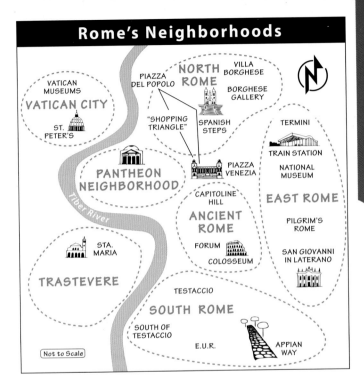

VATICAN MUSEUMS

VATICAN CITY

ST. PETER'S

PIAZZA DEL POPOLO

NORTH ROME

VILLA BORGHESE

BORGHESE GALLERY

"SHOPPING TRIANGLE"

SPANISH STEPS

TERMINI

TRAIN STATION

NATIONAL MUSEUM

PANTHEON NEIGHBORHOOD

PIAZZA VENEZIA

CAPITOLINE HILL

ANCIENT ROME

EAST ROME

PILGRIM'S ROME

Tiber River

FORUM

COLOSSEUM

SAN GIOVANNI IN LATERANO

STA. MARIA

TRASTEVERE

TESTACCIO

SOUTH ROME

SOUTH OF TESTACCIO

E.U.R.

APPIAN WAY

Not to Scale

buildings of a city of a million people. Today, the best of the classical sights stand in a line from the Colosseum to the Forum to the Pantheon.

Pantheon Neighborhood: The Pantheon anchors the neighborhood I like to call the "Heart of Rome." It stretches eastward from the Tiber River through Campo de' Fiori and Piazza Navona, past the Pantheon to the Trevi Fountain.

Vatican City: Located west of the Tiber, it's a compact world of its own, with two great, huge sights: St. Peter's Basilica and the Vatican Museums.

North Rome: With the Spanish Steps, Villa Borghese Gardens, and trendy shopping streets (Via Veneto and the "shopping triangle"), this is a more modern, classy area.

Key to This Book

Sights are rated:

▲▲▲ **Don't miss**
▲▲ **Try hard to see**
▲ **Worthwhile if you can make it**
No rating **Worth knowing about**

Tourist information offices are abbreviated as **TI** and bathrooms are **WCs**.

Like Europe, this book uses the **24-hour clock**. It's the same through 12:00 noon, then keep going: 13:00 (1:00 p.m.), 14:00 (2:00 p.m.), and so on.

For **opening times**, if a sight is listed as "May-Oct daily 9:00-16:00," it's open from 9 a.m. until 4 p.m. from the first day of May until the last day of October.

Trastevere: This colorful, wrong-side-of-the-river neighborhood has a village feel. South of Vatican City and just west of the Pantheon neighborhood, it's the city at its crustiest—and perhaps most "Roman."

Termini: Though light on sightseeing highlights, the train-station neighborhood has many recommended hotels and public-transportation connections.

Pilgrim's Rome: Several prominent churches dot the area south of Termini train station.

South Rome: Here are the postindustrial Testaccio neighborhood, the 1930s suburb of E.U.R., and the Appian Way, home of the catacombs.

Planning Your Time

The following day-plans give an idea of how much an organized, motivated, and caffeinated person can see. If you have less than a week, start with the Day 1 plan—the most important sights—and add on from there.

Day 1: The Colosseum is the ultimate place to begin your tour of ancient Rome. Then continue to the Forum and Pantheon. After a siesta, have dinner on atmospheric Campo de' Fiori, then take this book's Heart of Rome Walk to the Trevi Fountain and Spanish Steps. If all you have is this one day, skip the walk and see Day 2's sights in the afternoon and evening. Crazy as it sounds, many people actually "do" Rome in a day.

Daily Reminder

Sunday: These sights are closed—the Vatican Museums (except for the last Sunday of the month, when it's free and even more crowded), Villa Farnesina (except the second Sunday of the month), the Catacombs of San Sebastiano, and the Testaccio Market. In the morning, the Porta Portese flea market opens, and the old center is delightfully quiet. The Via dei Fori Imperiali and much of the Appian Way are closed to traffic and fun to stroll.

Monday: Many sights are closed, including the National Museum of Rome, Borghese Gallery, Montemartini Museum, Catacombs of Priscilla, Museum of the Imperial Forums, E.U.R.'s Museum of Roman Civilization (may be closed for renovation), Etruscan Museum, some Appian Way sights, Ostia Antica, and Villa d'Este (at Tivoli). Major sights that remain open include the Colosseum, Forum, and Vatican Museums. Churches are open.

Tuesday: All sights are open.

Wednesday: All sights are open, except for the Catacombs of San Callisto. St. Peter's Basilica is typically closed in the morning for a papal audience.

Thursday and Friday: All sights are open.

Saturday: Most sights are open, except the Synagogue and Jewish Museum.

Day 2: See St. Peter's, climb its dome, and tour the Vatican Museums. In the evening, join the locals strolling the Via del Corso *passeggiata*.

Day 3: See the Borghese Gallery (reservations required) and the Capitoline Museums.

Day 4: Take a side trip to Ostia Antica (closed Mon), the Appian Way, the Catacombs of Priscilla, or Tivoli.

Day 5: Visit the National Museum of Rome and walk through Trastevere.

Day 6: Visit the four churches of Pilgrim's Rome and the Capuchin Crypt.

Day 7: You choose—South Rome sights, St. Peter-in-Chains, Museo dell'Ara Pacis, Victor Emmanuel Monument viewpoint, Trajan's Column, shopping...or peruse the Sights chapter for more options.

Rome at a Glance

▲▲▲**Colosseum** Huge stadium where gladiators fought. **Hours:** Daily 8:30 until one hour before sunset: April-Aug until 19:15, Sept until 19:00, Oct until 18:30, off-season closes as early as 16:30. See page 13.

▲▲▲**Roman Forum** Ancient Rome's main square, with ruins and grand arches. **Hours:** Same hours as Colosseum. See page 27.

▲▲▲**Pantheon** The defining domed temple. **Hours:** Mon-Sat 8:30-19:30, Sun 9:00-18:00, holidays 9:00-13:00, closed for Mass Sat at 17:00 and Sun at 10:30. See page 132.

▲▲▲**Vatican Museums** Four miles of the finest art of Western civilization, culminating in Michelangelo's glorious Sistine Chapel. **Hours:** Mon-Sat 9:00-18:00. Closed on religious holidays and Sun, except last Sun of the month (open 9:00-14:00). Open Fri nights mid April-Oct by online reservation only. See page 53.

▲▲▲**St. Peter's Basilica** Most impressive church on earth, with Michelangelo's *Pietà* and dome. **Hours:** Church—daily April-Sept 7:00-19:00, Oct-March 7:00-18:30, often closed Wed mornings; dome—daily April-Sept 8:00-18:00, Oct-March 8:00-17:00. See page 81.

▲▲▲**Borghese Gallery** Bernini sculptures and paintings by Caravaggio, Raphael, and Titian in a Baroque palazzo. Reservations mandatory. **Hours:** Tue-Sun 9:00-19:00, closed Mon. See page 105.

▲▲▲**National Museum of Rome** Greatest collection of Roman sculpture anywhere. **Hours:** Tue-Sun 9:00-19:45, closed Mon. See page 137.

▲▲▲**Capitoline Museums** Ancient statues, mosaics, and expansive view of Forum. **Hours:** Daily 9:30-19:30. See page 129.

▲▲**Palatine Hill** Ruins of emperors' palaces, Circus Maximus view, and museum. **Hours:** Same hours as Colosseum. See page 122.

▲▲**Trajan's Column, Market, and Imperial Forums** Tall column with narrative relief, forum ruins, and museum with entry to Trajan's Market. **Hours:** Forum and column always viewable; museum open daily 9:30-19:30. See page 125.

▲▲**Museo dell'Ara Pacis** Shrine marking the beginning of Rome's Golden Age. **Hours:** Daily 9:30-19:30. See page 143.

▲▲**Catacombs** Underground tombs, mainly Christian. **Hours:** Generally open 10:00-12:00 & 14:00-17:00. See pages 144 and 153.

▲**St. Peter-in-Chains Church** with Michelangelo's *Moses*. **Hours:** Daily April-Sept 8:00-12:20 & 15:00-19:00, Oct-March until 18:00. See page 124.

▲**Piazza del Campidoglio** Square atop Capitoline Hill, designed by Michelangelo, with a museum, grand stairway, and Forum overlooks. **Hours:** Always open. See page 128.

▲**Victor Emmanuel Monument** Gigantic edifice celebrating Italian unity, with Rome from the Sky elevator ride up to 360-degree city view. **Hours:** Monument open daily 9:00-17:30, 9:30-16:30 in winter; elevator open daily until 19:30. See page 129.

▲**Galleria Doria Pamphilj** Aristocrat's ornate mansion shows off paintings by Caravaggio, Titian, and Raphael. **Hours:** Daily 9:00-19:00. See page 137.

▲**Trevi Fountain** Baroque hot spot into which tourists throw coins to ensure a return trip to Rome. **Hours:** Always flowing. See page 50.

▲**Baths of Diocletian/Basilica S. Maria degli Angeli** Once ancient Rome's immense public baths, now a Michelangelo church. **Hours:** Mon-Sat 7:00-18:30, Sun 7:00-19:30. See page 139.

▲**Santa Maria della Vittoria** Church with Bernini's swooning *St. Teresa in Ecstasy*. **Hours:** Mon-Sat 8:30-12:00 & 15:30-18:00, Sun 15:30-18:00. See page 140.

▲**Capuchin Crypt** Decorated with the bones of 4,000 Franciscan friars. **Hours:** Daily 9:00-19:00. See page 142.

▲**Castel Sant'Angelo** Hadrian's Tomb turned castle, prison, papal refuge, now museum. **Hours:** Daily 9:00-19:30. See page 145.

Introduction

Introduction

These are busy day-plans, so be sure to schedule in slack time for picnics, laundry, people-watching, shopping, hiding from the summer heat, and recharging your touristic batteries. Slow down and be open to unexpected experiences and the friendliness of Romans. Budget time for Rome after dark. Dine well at least once.

Quick Tips: Here are a few quick sightseeing tips to get you started—for more on these topics and other ideas, ✪ see page 195. Reservations are recommended for the Colosseum and the Vatican Museums and mandatory at the Borghese Gallery. Avoid lines at the Colosseum, St. Peter's, and elsewhere by following my suggestions. Since Rome's opening hours are notoriously variable, get the latest information from www.turismoroma.it and at tourist information offices (TIs) when you arrive. ∩ Take advantage of my free Rome audio tours, covering many of this book's sights.

And finally, remember that Rome has hosted visitors for 2,000 years with the same level of inefficiency, improvisation, and apathy you'll find today, so... be flexible. *Buon viaggio!*

Colosseum Tour

Colosseo

Start your visit to Rome with its iconic symbol—the Colosseum. Fifty thousand Romans could pack this huge stadium and cheer as their favorite gladiators faced off in bloody battles to the death.

This self-guided tour brings that ancient world to life—the world of Caesars, slaves, Vestal Virgins, trumpet fanfares, roaring lions, and hordes of rabid fans. Prowl the arena like gladiators, climb to the cheap seats for the view, see the underground "backstage" where they kept caged animals, and marvel at the engineering prowess that allowed these ancient people to build on such a colossal scale.

For its thrilling history and sheer massiveness, the Colosseum gets a unanimous thumbs-up.

ORIENTATION

Cost: A €12 combo-ticket covers the Colosseum and the Roman Forum/Palatine Hill. Buy it online well in advance to get a reserved Colosseum entry time (www.coopculture.it, extra €2 booking fee). The ticket is valid for two consecutive days; it allows one entry to the Colosseum and one entry to the Forum/Palatine Hill.

Hours: The Colosseum and the Roman Forum/Palatine Hill are open daily 8:30 until one hour before sunset: April-Aug until 19:15, Sept until 19:00, Oct until 18:30, Nov-mid-Feb until 16:30, mid-Feb-mid-March until 17:00, mid-March-late March until 17:30; last entry one hour before closing.

Information: Tel. 06-3996-7700, www.coopculture.it

Getting There: Metro: Colosseo, or buses #51, #75, #85, #87, and #118

Reservations and Avoiding Lines: Buy your ticket with a reserved-entry time online well in advance. If you show up without a reservation you can suffer in the long ticket-buying line or, as a last resort, join one of the tours sold by hawkers outside the gate. If you book a private tour in advance (see "Tours," below), the guide may be able to book your ticket and reservation. Warning: You may have to wait in a long line for security even with reservations.

Tours: A fact-filled audioguide is available just past the turnstiles (€5.50/1 hour) or videoguide (€6). Or ∩ download a free Rick Steves audio tour (✪ see page 195). Official guided tours in English depart roughly hourly (€5 plus Colosseum ticket, purchase inside Colosseum near ticket booth marked *Visite didattiche*). An interesting but not essential 1.5-hour guided tour ("Underground and Belvedere" tour) takes you through the otherwise off-limits underground passageways and third level (reserve ahead by phone or online; no same-day reservations). Private guides stand outside the Colosseum looking for business (€25-30 including Colosseum ticket).

Length of This Tour: Allow an hour.

Restoration: A multiyear renovation project may affect your visit.

Endless lines in the Eternal City

Goofy gladiators get two thumbs down.

THE TOUR BEGINS

▶ To enter, line up in the correct queue: the one for ticket buyers or the one for those who already have a ticket. The third line is for groups.

But before going inside, start by taking in the Colosseum's famous...

Exterior

Built when the Roman Empire was at its peak in A.D. 80, the Colosseum represents Rome at its grandest. The Flavian Amphitheater (the Colosseum's real name) was an arena for gladiator contests and public spectacles. When killing became a spectator sport, the Romans wanted to share the fun with as many people as possible, so they stuck two semicircular theaters together to create a freestanding amphitheater. The outside (where slender cypress trees stand today) was decorated with a 100-foot-tall bronze statue of Nero that gleamed in the sunlight. In a later age, the colossal structure was nicknamed a "coloss-eum," the wonder of its age. Towering 150 feet high, it could accommodate 50,000 roaring fans (100,000 thumbs).

The Romans pioneered the use of concrete and the rounded arch, which enabled them to build on this tremendous scale. The exterior is a skeleton of 3.5 million cubic feet of travertine stone. (Each of the pillars flanking the ground-level arches weighs five tons.) It took 200 ox-drawn wagons shuttling back and forth every day for four years just to bring the stone here from Tivoli. They stacked stone blocks (without mortar) into the shape of an arch, supported temporarily by wooden scaffolding. Finally,

Modern Amenities in the Ancient World

The area around the Colosseum, Forum, and Palatine Hill is rich in history, but pretty barren when it comes to food, shelter, and WCs. Here are a few options:

WCs: The Colosseum has a crowded WC inside. A WC is behind (east of) the structure (facing the ticket entrance, go clockwise; pay WC is under a stairway). The best WCs in the area are at Palatine Hill—at the main entrance, in the museum, outside the stadium, and in the Farnese Gardens. The Forum has WCs at the main entrance, near the Arch of Titus (in the "Soprintendenza" office), and in the middle of the Forum (near #6 on the map on ☉ page 29).

Buses: Except on Sundays, buses #51, #85, #87, #118, #186, and #810 stop along Via dei Fori Imperiali near the Colosseum entrance, one of the Forum/Palatine Hill entrances, and Piazza Venezia.

Eateries: You'll find a few restaurants behind the Colosseum (with expansive views of the structure), several recommended places within a few blocks (no views but better value), and some places near the Forum's main entrance—☉ see page 177. Or assemble a small picnic: The Colosseo Metro stop has €5 hot sandwiches, and snack stands on street corners sell drinks, sandwiches, fruit, and candy.

Water: Refill your water bottle at various public taps along city streets, as well as inside the Colosseum, Forum, and Palatine Hill.

Oases: The free tourist center, located across from the Forum entrance on Via dei Fori Imperiali and a bit east, has a small café, a WC, and a few exhibits. Atop **Capitoline Hill**, you'll find services at the Capitoline Museums, including a nice view café (☉ see page 129).

they wedged a keystone into the top of the arch—it not only kept the arch from falling, but could also bear even more weight above.

The exterior says a lot about the Romans. They were great engineers, not artists, and the building is more functional than beautiful. (If ancient Romans visited the US today as tourists, they might send home postcards of our greatest works of "art"—freeways.) While the essential structure of the Colosseum is Roman, the four-story facade is decorated with mostly

Greek columns—Doric-like Tuscan columns on the ground level, Ionic on the second story, Corinthian on the next level, and at the top, half-columns with a mix of all three. Originally, copies of Greek statues stood in the arches of the middle two stories, giving a veneer of sophistication to this arena of death.

Only a third of the original Colosseum remains. Earthquakes destroyed some of it. The pock-marks you see are the peg-holes for iron

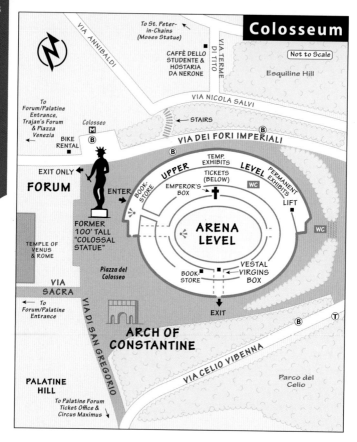

rods that stapled larger stones together. Most of the Colosseum's missing stones (along with the iron rods) were carted off during the Middle Ages and Renaissance and re-used to make other buildings that still adorn Rome today.

▶ *Once you're inside the structure, pass through the turnstiles. There may be signs directing you on a specific visitors' route, but eventually you'll be free to wander.*

Interior

Entering the Stadium

Imagine being an ancient spectator arriving for the games. Fans could pour in through ground-floor entrances; there were 76 numbered ones in addition to the emperor's private entrance on the north side. Your ticket (likely a piece of pottery) was marked with your entrance, section, row, and seat number. You'd pass by concession stands selling fast food and souvenirs, such as wine glasses with the names of famous gladiators. The hallways leading to the seats were called by the Latin word *vomitorium.* At exit time, the Colosseum would "vomit" out its contents, giving us the English word. It's estimated that 50,000 fans could enter and exit in 15 minutes.

▸ *Wherever you spill out into the arena—upstairs or downstairs, at one side of the arena or the other—just take it all in and get oriented. The tallest side of the Colosseum (with the large Christian cross) is the north side.*

Arena

The games took place in this oval-shaped arena, 280 feet long by 165 feet wide. The ratio of length to width is close to the so-called golden ratio. Since the days of the Greek mathematician Pythagoras, artists considered that proportion (1.6 to 1) to be ideal, with almost mystical properties. The Colosseum's architects may have wanted their structure to embody the perfect mathematical order they thought existed in nature.

When you look down into the arena, you're seeing the underground passages beneath the playing surface (which can only be visited on a private tour). The arena was originally covered with a wooden floor, and then sprinkled with sand (*arena* in Latin). The bit of reconstructed floor gives you an accurate sense of the original arena level, and the subterranean warren where animals and prisoners were held. As in modern stadiums, the spectators ringed the playing area in bleacher seats that slanted up from the arena floor. Around you are the big brick masses that supported the tiers of seats.

A variety of materials were used to build the stadium. Look around. Big white travertine blocks stacked on top of each other formed the skeleton. The pillars for the bleachers were made with a shell of brick, filled in

Column capital of marble

The top story once held an awning.

with concrete. Originally the bare brick was covered with marble columns or ornamental facing, so the interior was a brilliant white (they used white plaster for the upper-floor cheap seats).

Looking into the complex web of passageways beneath the arena, you can imagine how busy the backstage action was. Gladiators strolled down the central passageway, from their warm-up yard on the east end to the arena entrance on the west. Some workers tended wild animals. Others prepared stage sets of trees or fake buildings, transforming the arena into an African jungle or Greek temple. Props and sets were hauled up to arena level on 80 different elevator shafts via a system of ropes and pulleys. (You might be able to make out some small rectangular shafts, especially near the center of the arena.) That means there were 80 different spots from which animals, warriors, and stage sets could magically appear.

The Seating

The Colosseum's seating was strictly segregated. At ringside, the emperor, senators, Vestal Virgins, and VIPs occupied marble seats with their names carved on them (a few marble seats have been restored, at the east end). The next level upheld those of noble birth. The level tourists now occupy was for ordinary free Roman citizens, called plebeians. Up at the very top (a hundred yards from the action), there were once wooden bleachers for the poorest people—foreigners, slaves, and women.

The top story of the Colosseum is mostly ruined—only the north side still retains its high wall. This was not part of the original three-story structure, but was added around A.D. 230 after a fire. Picture the awning that could be stretched across the top of the stadium by armies of sailors.

Strung along horizontal beams that pointed inward to the center, the awning only covered about a third of the arena—so those at the top always enjoyed shade, while many nobles down below roasted in the sun.

The Games

The games began with a few warm-up acts—dogs bloodying themselves attacking porcupines, female gladiators fighting each other, or a one-legged man battling a dwarf. Then came the main event—the gladiators.

"Hail, Caesar! *(Ave, Caesar!)* We who are about to die salute you!" The gladiators would enter the arena from the west end, parade around to the sound of trumpets, acknowledge the Vestal Virgins (on the south side), then stop at the emperor's box (supposedly marked today by the cross that stands at the "50-yard line" on the north side—although no one knows for sure where it was). They would then raise their weapons, shout, and salute—and begin fighting. The fights pitted men against men, men against beasts, and beasts against beasts. Picture 50,000 screaming people around you (did gladiators get stage fright?), and imagine that they want to see you die.

The arena had underground passageways, where gladiators warmed up amid caged animals.

A Page of History

Ancient Rome (500 B.C.- A.D. 500): Legend says that Romulus and Remus—twins orphaned at birth and raised by a she-wolf—founded Rome in 753 B.C. From humble beginnings, the city expanded, through conquest and trade, to dominate the Italian peninsula and beyond.

By A.D. 100, Rome was master of Western Europe and the Mediterranean. Booty and captured slaves poured in. The former Republic (governed by a senate) was now an empire of 54 million people. The city of Rome, population 1.2 million, was dotted with monumental sports stadiums, baths, aqueducts, and temples—the wonder of the age.

Corruption, disease, and barbarian attacks slowly drained the unwieldy empire. Though Emperor Constantine brought temporary stability and legalized Christianity (in 313), Rome eventually fell to invaders (A.D. 476), plunging Europe into chaos.

Medieval (A.D. 500-1500): The once-great city dwindled to a rough village of overgrown ruins. During the 1300s, even the popes left Rome to live in France. What little glory Rome retained was in the pomp, knowledge, and wealth of the Catholic Church.

Renaissance (1500s): As Europe's economy recovered, energetic popes rebuilt Rome, including the new St. Peter's Basilica.

Baroque and Neoclassical (1600-1900): The city was no longer a great political force, but it remained the influential capital of Catholicism during the struggle against Protestants. To attract pilgrims, popes further beautified the city, in the Baroque and Neoclassical styles: St. Peter's Square, ornate church interiors, Bernini's statues, and the Trevi Fountain. In 1871, modern Italy was formed under King Victor Emmanuel II, and—naturally—Rome was named its capital.

War, Fascism, Revival (1900s): Italy's fascist dictator Benito Mussolini modernized Rome with broad boulevards and the Metro system. He also dragged Italy into WWII's destruction, though the city's monuments were spared. Postwar Italy suffered through government-a-year chaos and Mafia-tainted corruption. But its "economic miracle" made Rome a world-class city of cinema (Fellini), banking, and tourism.

Rome Today: Today, the average Roman makes more money than the average Englishman. The city's monuments are spruced up and the economy hums. Rome is ready for pilgrims, travelers...and you.

Some gladiators wielded swords, protected only with a shield and a heavy helmet. Others represented fighting fishermen, with a net to snare opponents and a trident to spear them. The gladiators were usually slaves, criminals, or poor people who got their chance for freedom, wealth, and fame in the ring. They learned to fight in training schools, then battled their way up the ranks. The best were rewarded like our modern sports stars, with fan clubs, great wealth, and, yes, product endorsements.

The animals were imported from all over the world: lions, tigers, and bears (oh my!), crocodiles, elephants, and hippos (not to mention exotic human "animals" from the "barbarian" lands). They were kept in cages beneath the arena floor, and then lifted up in the elevators. Released at floor level, animals would pop out from behind blinds into the arena—the gladiator didn't know where, when, or by what he'd be attacked. Many a hapless warrior met his death here, and never knew what hit him. (This sometimes brought howls of laughter from the hardened fans in the cheap upper seats who had a better view of the action.)

Nets ringed the arena to protect the crowd. The stadium was inaugurated with a 100-day festival in which 2,000 men and 9,000 animals were killed. Colosseum employees squirted perfumes around the stadium to mask the stench of blood.

If a gladiator fell helpless to the ground, his opponent would approach the emperor's box and ask: Should he live or die? Sometimes the emperor left the decision to the crowd, who would judge based on how valiantly the man had fought. They would make their decision: thumbs-up or thumbs-down.

Did they throw Christians to the lions like in the movies? Christians were definitely thrown to the lions, made to fight gladiators, crucified, and burned alive...but probably not here in this particular stadium.

Why were the Romans so bloodthirsty? Consider the value of these games in placating and controlling the huge Roman populace. Seeing Germanic barbarians or African lions slain by a gladiator reminded the citizens of civilized Rome's conquest of distant lands. And having the thumbs-up or thumbs-down authority over another person's life gave the downtrodden masses a sense of power. Once a nation of warriors, Rome became a nation of bureaucrats, who got vicarious thrills by watching brutes battle to the death. The contests were always free, sponsored by the government to bribe the people's favor or to keep Rome's growing masses of unemployed rabble off the streets.

▶ *With these scenes in mind, wander around, and then check out the*

A cross marks the emperor's box.

Arch of Constantine—Christianity triumphs

upper level. Stairs are on both the east and west sides, with an elevator at the east end (only accessible to those who really need it). The upper deck offers more colossal views of the arena, plus a bookstore and temporary exhibits. Wherever you may Rome, find a spot at the west end of the upper deck, where you can look out over some of the sights nearby. Start with the big, white, triumphal Arch of Constantine.

Views from the Upper Level

Arch of Constantine

If you are a Christian, were raised a Christian, or simply belong to a so-called "Christian nation," ponder this arch. It marks one of the great turning points in history—the military coup that made Christianity mainstream.

In A.D. 312, Emperor Constantine defeated his rival Maxentius in the crucial Battle of the Milvian Bridge. The night before, he had seen a vision of a cross in the sky. Constantine—whose mother and sister were Christians—became sole emperor and legalized Christianity. With this one battle, a once-obscure Jewish sect with a handful of followers was now the state religion of the entire Western world. In A.D. 300, you could be killed for being a Christian; a century later, you could be killed for not being one. Church enrollment boomed.

The arch trumpets the legitimacy of Constantine's rule by including glorious emperors that came before. Hadrian is in the round reliefs, Marcus Aurelius in the square reliefs, and statues of Trajan and Augustus adorn the top. Originally, Augustus drove a chariot similar to the one topping the modern Victor Emmanuel II Monument. Fourth-century Rome may have been in decline, but Constantine clung to its glorious past.

Surrounding Hills

The Colosseum stands in a valley between three of Rome's legendary seven hills. Palatine Hill rises to the southwest, beyond the Arch of Constantine, dotted with umbrella pines. The Caelian is to the south and the Esquiline is to the north. Next to the Arch of Constantine is the road called the Via Sacra, or Sacred Way, once Rome's main street, that leads uphill from the Colosseum to the Forum.

▶ *Looking west, in the direction of the Forum, you'll see some ruins sitting atop a raised, rectangular-shaped hill. The ruins—consisting of an arched alcove made of brick and backed by a church bell tower—are all that remain of the once great Temple of Venus and Rome.*

The Temple of Venus and Rome

Rome's biggest temple could be seen from almost everywhere in the city. The size of a football field, it covered the entire hill, surrounded by white columns, six feet thick.

The main ruin in the center—the tall brick arch with a cross-hatched

Temple of Venus and Rome

ceiling—was once the temple's *cella,* or sacred chamber. Here sat two monumental statues, back to back—Venus, the goddess of Love (Amor in Latin), and the city's patron (Roma). Roma and Amor—a perfectly symmetrical palindrome—showing how love and the city were meant to go together. In ancient times, newlyweds ascended the staircase from the Colosseum (some parts are still visible) to the temple, to ask the twin goddesses to bring them good luck. These days, Roman couples get married at the church with the bell tower to ensure themselves love and happiness for eternity.

The Colosseum's Legacy: A.D. 500 to the Present

With the coming of Christianity to Rome, the Colosseum and its deadly games slowly became politically incorrect. The stadium was neglected as the Roman Empire dwindled and the infrastructure crumbled. Around A.D. 523—after nearly 500 years of games—the last animal was slaughtered, and the Colosseum shut its doors.

For the next thousand years, the structure was used by various squatters, as a makeshift church, and as a refuge during invasions and riots. Over time, the Colosseum was eroded by wind, rain, and the strain of gravity. Earthquakes weakened it, and a powerful quake in 1349 toppled the south side.

More than anything, the Colosseum was dismantled by the Roman citizens themselves, who carted off precut stones to be re-used for palaces and churches, including St. Peter's. The marble facing was pulverized into mortar, and 300 tons of iron brackets were pried out and melted down, resulting in the pockmarking you see today.

After centuries of neglect, a series of 16th-century popes took pity on the pagan structure. In memory of the Christians who may (or may not) have been martyred here, they shored up the south and west sides with bricks and placed the big cross on the north side of the arena.

Today, the Colosseum links Rome's glorious past with its vital present. Major political demonstrations begin or end here, providing protestors with an iconic backdrop for the TV cameras. On Good Fridays, the pope comes here to lead pilgrims as they follow the Stations of the Cross.

The legend goes that so long as the Colosseum shall stand, the city of Rome shall also stand. For nearly 2,000 years, the Colosseum has been the enduring symbol of the Eternal City.

Roman Forum Tour

Foro Romano

For nearly a thousand years, the Forum was the vital heart of Rome. Nestled in Rome's famous seven hills, this is the Eternal City's birthplace. While only broken columns and arches remain of the Forum today, this tour helps resurrect the rubble.

Stroll down main street, where shoppers in togas once came to browse and gawk at towering temples and triumphal arches. See where senators passed laws and where orators mounted a rostrum to address their friends, Romans, and countrymen. Visit the temple where Vestal Virgins tended a sacred flame and the spot where Julius Caesar's body was burned. In the middle of it all, you'll still find the main square where ancient citizens once passed the time, just as Romans do in piazzas today.

ORIENTATION

Cost: €12 combo-ticket covers the Colosseum/Forum/Palatine Hill. Buy your ticket online well in advance for a reserved Colosseum entry time (www.coopculture.it, €2 booking fee, tickets valid two consecutive days). The €16 "SUPER" combo-ticket sold on-site covers the Forum/Palatine Hill and extras—but not the Colosseum.

Hours: The Roman Forum/Palatine Hill and Colosseum are open daily 8:30 until one hour before sunset: April-Aug until 19:15, Sept until 19:00, Oct until 18:30, off-season closes as early as 16:30; last entry one hour before closing.

Information: Tel. 06-3996-7700, www.coopculture.it. A free information center is 100 yards east of the entrance on Via dei Fori Imperiali (daily 9:30-19:00).

Getting In: There are three main entrances: 1) from the Colosseum—nearest the Arch of Titus; 2) from Via dei Fori Imperiali; and 3) from Via di San Gregorio—at south end of Palatine Hill. See map for details.

Tours: An unexciting yet informative audioguide helps decipher the rubble (€5/2 hours, €7 version includes Palatine Hill). Or ⌂ download a free Rick Steves audio tour of the Forum (✪ see page 195).

Length of This Tour: Allow 1.5 hours.

Services: For information on food and WCs in the area, ✪ see page 16.

Roman Forum

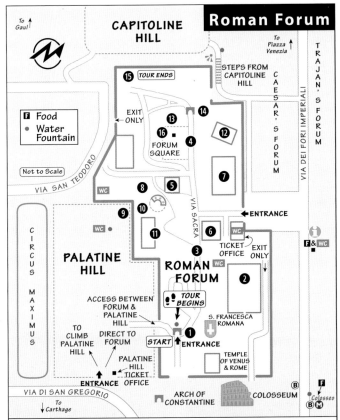

To Gaul

CAPITOLINE HILL

To Piazza Venezia

STEPS FROM CAPITOLINE HILL

TOUR ENDS ⑮

EXIT ONLY

⑬ ⑭

⑯

FORUM SQUARE ④

⑫

🅵 Food
• Water Fountain

Not to Scale

VIA SAN TEODORO

WC ⑧ ⑤

⑨ ⑩ ⑦

WC ⑪

C I R C U S   M A X I M U S

PALATINE HILL

VIA SACRA

◄ ENTRANCE

⑥

WC

TICKET OFFICE   **EXIT ONLY**

ROMAN FORUM WC

② 🅵 & WC

ACCESS BETWEEN FORUM & PALATINE HILL

● **TOUR BEGINS**

S. FRANCESCA ROMANA

TO CLIMB PALATINE HILL   **DIRECT TO FORUM**

① **START** ↑ **ENTRANCE**

PALATINE HILL TICKET OFFICE

ENTRANCE

TEMPLE OF VENUS & ROME

VIA DI SAN GREGORIO

To Carthage

ARCH OF CONSTANTINE   **COLOSSEUM** 🅱

🅱 Ⓜ

🅵 Colosseo

C A E S A R ' S   F O R U M

T R A J A N ' S   F O R U M

VIA DEI FORI IMPERIALI

① Arch of Titus	⑨ Caligula's Palace
② Basilica of Constantine	⑩ Temple of Vesta
③ Via Sacra	⑪ House of the Vestal Virgins
④ The Forum's Main Square	⑫ The Curia
⑤ Temple of Julius Caesar	⑬ Rostrum
⑥ Temple of Antoninus Pius & Faustina	⑭ Arch of Septimius Severus
⑦ Basilica Aemilia	⑮ Temple of Saturn

THE TOUR BEGINS

▶ *Start at the Arch of Titus. It's the white triumphal arch that rises above the rubble on the east end of the Forum (closest to the Colosseum). Stand alongside the arch and gaze over the valley known as the Forum.*

Overview

The Forum is a rectangular valley running roughly east (the Colosseum end) to west (Capitoline Hill, with its bell tower). The rocky path at your feet is the Via Sacra. It leads from the Arch of Titus, through the trees, past the large brick Senate building, through the triumphal arch at the far end, and up Capitoline Hill. The hill to your left (with all the trees) is Palatine Hill.

Picture being here when a conquering general returned to Rome with crates of booty. The valley was full of gleaming white buildings topped with bronze roofs. The Via Sacra—the Forum's Main Street—would be lined with citizens waving branches and carrying torches. The trumpets would sound as the parade began.

The overgrown rubble of the Forum is nestled in a valley at the base of Capitoline Hill.

Rome: Republic and Empire (500 B.C.–A.D. 500)

Ancient Rome lasted for a thousand years, from about 500 B.C. to A.D. 500. During that time, Rome expanded from a small tribe of barbarians to a vast empire, then dwindled slowly to city size again. For the first 500 years, when Rome's armies made her ruler of the Italian peninsula and beyond, Rome was a republic governed by elected senators. Over the next 500 years, a time of world conquest and eventual decline, Rome was an empire ruled by a military-backed dictator.

Julius Caesar bridged the gap between republic and empire. This ambitious general and politician, popular with the people because of his military victories and charisma, suspended the Roman constitution and assumed dictatorial powers in about 50 B.C. A few years later, he was assassinated by a conspiracy of senators. His adopted son, Augustus, succeeded him, and soon "Caesar" was not just a name but a title.

Emperor Augustus ushered in the Pax Romana, or Roman peace (A.D. 1-200), a time when Rome reached her peak and controlled an empire that stretched even beyond Eurail—from England to Egypt, Turkey to Morocco.

First came porters, carrying chests full of gold and jewels. Then, a parade of exotic animals from the conquered lands—elephants, giraffes, hippopotamuses—for the crowd to "ooh" and "ahh" at. Next came the prisoners in chains, with the captive king on a wheeled platform so the people could jeer and spit at him. Finally, the conquering hero himself would drive down in his four-horse chariot, with rose petals strewn in his path.

The procession would run the length of the Forum and up the face of Capitoline Hill to the Temple of Saturn (the eight big columns midway up the hill—#14 on the map), where they'd place the booty in Rome's coffers. Then they'd continue up to the summit to the Temple of Jupiter (only ruined foundations remain today) to dedicate the victory to the King of the Gods.

❶ Arch of Titus (Arco di Tito)

The Arch of Titus commemorated the Roman victory over the province of Judaea (Israel) in A.D. 70. The Romans had a reputation as benevolent conquerors who tolerated the local customs and rulers. All they required was allegiance to the empire, shown by worshipping the emperor as a god. No problem for most conquered people, who already had half a dozen gods on their prayer lists anyway. But Israelites believed in only one god, and it wasn't the emperor. Israel revolted. After a short but bitter war, the Romans defeated the rebels, took Jerusalem, destroyed their temple (leaving only the foundation wall—today's revered "Wailing Wall"), and brought home 50,000 Jewish slaves...who were forced to build the Colosseum and this arch.

Roman propaganda decorates the inside of the arch, where a relief shows the emperor Titus in a chariot being crowned by the goddess Victory. (Thanks to modern pollution, they both look like they've been through the wars.) The other side shows booty from the sacking of the temple in Jerusalem—soldiers carrying a Jewish menorah and other plunder. The two (unfinished) plaques on poles were to have listed the conquered cities. Look at the top of the ceiling. Carved after Titus' death, the relief shows him riding an eagle to heaven, where he'll become one of the gods.

The brutal crushing of the A.D. 70 rebellion (and another one 60 years

After Titus conquered the Jews, he made them build his victory monument—the Arch of Titus.

later) devastated the nation of Israel. With no temple as a center for their faith, the Jews scattered throughout the world (the Diaspora). There would be no Jewish political entity again for almost 2,000 years, until modern Israel was created after World War II.

► *Walk down the Via Sacra into the Forum. After about 50 yards, turn right and follow a path uphill to the three huge arches of the...*

❷ Basilica of Constantine (a.k.a. Basilica Maxentius)

Yes, these are big arches. But they represent only one-third of the original Basilica of Constantine, a mammoth hall of justice. The arches were matched by a similar set along the Via Sacra side, where only a few squat brick piers remain. Between them ran the central hall, which was spanned by a roof 130 feet high—about 55 feet higher than the side arches you see. (The stub of brick you see sticking up began an arch that once spanned the central hall.)

The hall itself was as long as a football field, lavishly furnished with colorful inlaid marble, a gilded bronze ceiling, and statues, and filled with strolling Romans. At the far (west) end was an enormous marble statue of Emperor Constantine on a throne. Pieces of this statue, including a hand the size of a man, are on display in Rome's Capitoline Museums.

No doubt about it, the Romans built monuments on a more epic scale than any previous Europeans, wowing their "barbarian" neighbors.

► *Now stroll deeper into the Forum, downhill along Via Sacra, through the trees. Many of the large basalt stones under your feet were walked on by Caesar Augustus 2,000 years ago. Pass by the Tempio di Romolo (on the right) with its original bronze door, and continue between ruined buildings until the Via Sacra opens up to a flat, grassy area.*

These arches are all that remain...

...of the once-grand Basilica of Constantine.

Today's field of rubble...

...was once a gleaming canyon of marble.

❸ The Forum's Main Square

The original Forum, or main square, was this flat patch about the size of a football field, stretching to the foot of Capitoline Hill. Surrounding it were temples, law courts, government buildings, and triumphal arches.

Rome was born right here. According to legend, twin brothers Romulus (Rome) and Remus were orphaned in infancy and raised by a she-wolf on top of Palatine Hill. Growing up, they found it hard to get dates. So they and their cohorts attacked the nearby Sabine tribe and kidnapped their women. After they made peace, this marshy valley became the trading center for the scattered tribes on the surrounding hillsides.

The square was the busiest and most crowded—and often the seediest—section of town. Besides the senators, politicians, and currency exchangers, there were even sleazier typos souvenir hawkers, pickpockets, fortune-tellers, gamblers, slave marketers, drunks, hookers, lawyers, and tour guides.

Ancient Rome's population exceeded one million, a teeming mass crammed into tiny apartments. The public space—their Forum, today's piazza—is where they did their living. Consider how, to this day, the piazza is still such an important part of any Italian town. Since Roman times, the piazza has reflected and accommodated the gregarious and outgoing nature of the Italian people.

The Forum is now rubble, but imagine it in its prime: blindingly brilliant marble buildings with 40-foot-high columns and shining bronze roofs; rows of statues painted in realistic colors; processional chariots rattling down Via Sacra. Mentally replace tourists in T-shirts with tribunes in togas. Imagine the buildings towering and the people buzzing around you while an orator gives a rabble-rousing speech from the Rostrum. If things still

Religion in Ancient Rome

Religion in ancient Rome was all about the *pax deorum* (peace, or pact, with the gods) that guaranteed the prosperity of the incredibly superstitious Romans. To appease the fickle gods they performed elaborate rituals at lavish temples and shrines. Priests interpreted the will of the gods by studying the internal organs of sacrificed animals, the flight of birds, and prophetic books. A clap of thunder was enough to postpone a battle.

Astrology, magic rites, the cult of deified emperors, house gods, and the near-deification of ancestors permeated Roman life. But all these practices were gradually replaced when Emperor Constantine embraced Christianity in A.D. 313. By 390, the Christian God was the only legal god in Rome.

look like just a pile of rocks, tell yourself, "But Julius Caesar once leaned against these rocks."

▶ *At the near end of the main square are the foundations of a temple now capped with a peaked wood-and-metal roof.*

❹ Temple of Julius Caesar (Tempio del Divo Giulio, or Ara di Cesare)

On March 15, in 44 B.C., Julius Caesar was stabbed 23 times by political conspirators. After his assassination, Caesar's body was cremated on this spot (under the metal roof) and this temple was built to honor him. Peek behind the wall into the small apse area, where a mound of dirt usually has fresh flowers—left here to remember the man who, more than any other, personified the greatness of Rome.

Caesar (100-44 B.C.) changed Rome—and the Forum—dramatically. He cleared out many of the wooden market stalls and began to ring the square with even grander buildings. Caesar's house was located behind the temple, near that clump of trees. He walked right by here on the day he was assassinated ("Beware the Ides of March!" warned a street-corner Etruscan preacher).

Though he was popular with the masses, not everyone liked Caesar's urban design or his politics. When he assumed dictatorial powers, he was ambushed and stabbed to death by a conspiracy of senators, including his adopted son, Brutus *("Et tu, Brute?")*.

The funeral was held here, facing the main square. The citizens gathered, and speeches were made. Mark Antony stood up to say (in Shakespeare's words), "Friends, Romans, countrymen, lend me your ears. I come to bury Caesar, not to praise him." When Caesar's body was burned, his adoring fans threw anything at hand on the fire, requiring the fire department to come put it out. Later, Emperor Augustus dedicated this temple in his name, making Caesar the first Roman to become a god.

▶ *Behind and to the left of the Temple of Julius Caesar are the 10 tall columns of the...*

❺ Temple of Antoninus Pius and Faustina

The Senate built this temple to honor Emperor Antoninus Pius (A.D. 138-161) and his deified wife, Faustina. The 50-foot-tall Corinthian (leafy) columns must have been awe-inspiring to out-of-towners who grew up in thatched huts. Notice the basic temple layout—a staircase led to a shaded porch

The Temple of Antoninus Pius and Faustina gives a glimpse at the Forum's former grandeur.

(the columns), which admitted you to the main building (now a church), where the statue of the god sat. Originally, these columns supported a triangular pediment decorated with sculptures.

Picture these columns, with gilded capitals, supporting brightly painted statues in the pediment, and the whole building capped with a gleaming bronze roof. The stately gray rubble of today's Forum is a faded black-and-white photograph of a 3-D Technicolor era.

▸ *The ruins of the Basilica Aemilia can be viewed from the ramp next to the Temple of Antoninus Pius and Faustina. (Or find the entrance near the Curia.)*

⑥ Basilica Aemilia

The word "basilica" originally meant a covered public forum, often serving as a Roman hall of justice. In a society that was as legal-minded as America is today, you needed a lot of lawyers—and a big place to put them. Citizens came here to work out matters such as inheritances and building permits, or to sue somebody.

Notice the layout. It was a long, rectangular building. The stubby columns all in a row form one long, central hall flanked by two side aisles. Medieval Christians required a larger meeting hall for their worship services than Roman temples provided, so they used the spacious Roman basilica as the model for their churches. Cathedrals from France to Spain to England, from Romanesque to Gothic to Renaissance, all have the same basic floor plan, and are often called by the same Latin word—basilica.

▸ *Return again to the Temple of Julius Caesar. To the right of the temple are the three tall Corinthian columns of the...*

⑦ Temple of Castor and Pollux

These three columns—all that remain of one of the Forum's most prestigious temples (fifth-century B.C.)—have become the most photographed sight in the Forum. The temple commemorated the Roman victory over Tarquin, the notorious Etruscan king who oppressed them. As a symbol of Rome's self-governing Republic, the temple was often used as a meeting place of senators, and its front steps served as a podium for free speech.

From here, gaze beyond the three columns to Palatine Hill, the corner of which may have been ⑧ **Caligula's Palace** (a.k.a. the Palace of Tiberius). Emperor Caligula (ruled A.D. 37-41) had a huge palace on Palatine Hill overlooking the Forum. It actually sprawled down the hillside (where

Temple of Castor and Pollux

Temple of Vesta, tended by Vestal Virgins

a few supporting arches remain) into the Forum. Caligula was not a nice person. He tortured enemies, stole senators' wives, and parked his chariot in handicap spaces. But Rome's luxury-loving emperors only added to the glory of the Forum, with each one trying to make his mark on history.

▶ *To the left of the Temple of Castor and Pollux, find the remains of a small, white circular temple.*

9 Temple of Vesta

This is perhaps Rome's most sacred spot. Rome considered itself one big family, and this temple represented a circular hut, like the kind that Rome's first families lived in. Inside, a fire burned, just as in a Roman home. And back in the days before lighters and butane, you never wanted your fire to go out. As long as the sacred flame burned, Rome would stand. The flame was tended by priestesses known as Vestal Virgins.

Just to the left and up the stairs is a big, enclosed field with two rectangular brick pools (just below the hill). This was the courtyard of the...

10 House of the Vestal Virgins

The Vestal Virgins lived in a two-story building surrounding a long central courtyard with these two pools at one end. Rows of statues depicting leading Vestal Virgins flanked the courtyard. This place was the model— both architecturally and sexually—for medieval convents and monasteries.

Chosen from noble families before they reached the age of 10, the six Vestal Virgins served a 30-year term. Honored and revered by the Romans, the Vestals even had their own box opposite the emperor in the Colosseum.

As the name implies, a Vestal took a vow of chastity. If she served her term faithfully—abstaining for 30 years—she was given a huge dowry, and allowed to marry. But if they found any Virgin who wasn't, she was strapped to a funeral car, paraded through the streets of the Forum, taken to a crypt, given a loaf of bread and a lamp...and buried alive. Many women suffered the latter fate.

▶ *Return to the Temple of Julius Caesar and head to the Forum's west end (opposite from the Colosseum). Stop at the big, well-preserved brick building (on right) with the triangular roof—the Curia. (Ongoing archaeological work may restrict access to the Curia and surrounding structures.)*

⑪ The Curia (Senate House)

The Curia was the most important political building in the Forum. While the present building dates from A.D. 283, this was the site of Rome's official center of government since the birth of the republic. Three hundred senators, elected by the citizens of Rome, met here to debate and create the laws of the land. Their wooden seats once circled the building in three tiers; the Senate president's podium sat at the far end. The marble floor is from ancient times. Listen to the echoes in this vast room—the acoustics are great.

Rome prided itself on being a republic. Early in the city's history, its people threw out the king and established rule by elected representatives. Each Roman citizen was free to speak his mind and have a say in public policy. Even when emperors became the supreme authority, the Senate was a power to be reckoned with. The Curia building is well-preserved, having been used as a church since early Christian times. Note: Although Julius Caesar was assassinated in "the Senate," it wasn't here—the Senate was temporarily meeting across town.

▶ *Go back down the Senate steps and find the 10-foot-high wall just to the left of the big arch, marked...*

⑫ Rostrum (Rostri)

Nowhere was Roman freedom more apparent than at this "Speaker's Corner." The Rostrum was a raised platform, 10 feet high and 80 feet long, decorated with statues, columns, and the prows of ships (rostra).

On a stage like this, Rome's orators, great and small, tried to draw a crowd and sway public opinion. Mark Antony rose to offer Caesar the laurel-leaf crown of kingship, which Caesar publicly (and hypocritically) refused while privately becoming a dictator. Cicero railed against the corruption and decadence that came with the city's newfound wealth. In later years, daring citizens even spoke out against the emperors, reminding them that Rome was once free. Picture the backdrop these speakers would have had—a mountain of marble buildings piling up on Capitoline Hill.

In front of the Rostrum are trees bearing fruits that were sacred to the ancient Romans: olives (provided food, light, and preservatives), figs (tasty), and wine grapes (for a popular export product).

▶ *The big arch to the right of the Rostrum is the...*

⓭ Arch of Septimius Severus

In imperial times, the Rostrum's voices of democracy would have been dwarfed by images of the empire, such as the huge six-story-high Arch of Septimius Severus (A.D. 203). The reliefs commemorate the African-born emperor's battles in Mesopotamia. Near ground level, see soldiers marching captured barbarians back to Rome for the victory parade. Despite Severus' efficient rule, Rome's empire was crumbling.

Arch of Septimius Severus—one of the Forum's later monuments, before Rome's long decline

Temple of Saturn—the Forum's oldest temple, on the flank of Capitoline Hill

▶ *Pass beneath the Arch of Septimius Severus and turn left. On the slope of Capitoline Hill are the eight remaining columns of the...*

⑭ Temple of Saturn

These columns framed the entrance to the Forum's oldest temple (497 B.C.). Inside was a humble, very old wooden statue of the god Saturn. But the statue's pedestal held the gold bars, coins, and jewels of Rome's state treasury, the booty collected by conquering generals.

▶ *Standing here, at one of the Forum's first buildings, look east at the lone, tall...*

⑮ Column of Phocas—Rome's Fall

This is the Forum's last monument (A.D. 608), a gift from the powerful Byzantine Empire to a fallen empire—Rome. Given to commemorate the pagan Pantheon's becoming a Christian church, it's like a symbolic last nail in ancient Rome's coffin.

After Rome's 1,000-year reign, the city was looted by Vandals, the population of a million-plus shrank to about 10,000, and the once-grand city center—the Forum—was abandoned, slowly covered up by centuries of silt and dirt. In the 1700s, an English historian named Edward Gibbon

Rome Falls

Remember that Rome lasted 1,000 years—500 years of growth, 200 years of peak power, and 300 years of gradual decay. The fall had many causes—corruption, plagues, crumbling infrastructure, and a false economy based on spoils of war. On the borders, barbarian tribes poured in, pushing the Roman legions back. The Europe-wide empire gradually shrank to little more than the city of Rome. In A.D. 410, barbarians even looted Rome itself, leveling many of the buildings in the Forum. In 476, the last emperor checked out, switched off the lights, and plunged Europe into centuries of poverty, ignorance, superstition, and hand-me-down leotards—the Dark Ages.

But Rome lived on in the Catholic Church. Christianity was the state religion of Rome's last generations. Emperors became popes (both called themselves "Pontifex Maximus"), senators became bishops, orators became priests, and basilicas became churches. The glory of Rome remains eternal.

overlooked this spot from Capitoline Hill. Hearing Christian monks singing at these pagan ruins, he looked out at the few columns poking up from the ground, pondered the decline and fall of the Roman Empire, and thought, "Hmm, that's a catchy title...."

▶ *There are several ways to exit the Forum:*

1. Near the Arch of Septimius Severus are stairs that lead up to Capitoline Hill.

2. The Forum's main entrance spills you back out onto Via dei Fori Imperiali.

3. From the Arch of Titus, you can climb and tour Palatine Hill (for details, ✪ see page 122).

4. Exiting past the Arch of Titus lands you at the Colosseum.

Heart of Rome Walk

From Campo de' Fiori to the Spanish Steps

Rome's most colorful neighborhood features narrow lanes, intimate piazzas, fanciful fountains, and some of Europe's best people-watching. During the day, this walk shows off the colorful Campo de' Fiori market and trendy fashion boutiques as it meanders past major monuments such as the Pantheon and the Spanish Steps.

But the sunset brings unexpected magic. Sit so close to a bubbling fountain that traffic noise evaporates. Jostle with kids to see the gelato flavors. Watch lovers straddling more than the bench. And marvel at the ramshackle elegance that softens this brutal city. These are the flavors of Rome, best tasted after dark.

THE WALK BEGINS

▶ *Start this mile-long walk at the Campo de' Fiori. The transportation hub Largo Argentina (buses #40, #64, #492, tram #8, and taxis) is five blocks west. This walk is equally pleasant in reverse order: start at Metro: Spanish Steps and finish at Campo de' Fiori, my favorite outdoor dining room after dark—for recommendations, ✪ see page 175. My free ♎ Rick Steves audio tour covers a longer walk than the one described here.*

Campo de' Fiori

One of Rome's most colorful spots, this bohemian piazza hosts a fruit and vegetable market in the morning, cafés in the evening, and pub-crawlers at night. In ancient times, the "Field of Flowers" was an open meadow. Later, Christian pilgrims passed through on their way to the Vatican, and a thriving market developed.

Lording over the center of the square is a statue of Giordano Bruno,

Campo de' Fiori's raucous morning market, overseen by the statue of the rebel Giordano Bruno

an intellectual heretic who was burned on this spot in 1600. The pedestal shows scenes from Bruno's trial and execution, and reads, "And the flames rose up." When this statue honoring a heretic was erected in 1889, the Vatican protested, but they were overruled by angry Campo locals. The neighborhood is still known for its free spirit and antiauthoritarian demonstrations.

Campo de' Fiori is the product of centuries of unplanned urban development. At the east end of the square (behind Bruno), the ramshackle apartments are built right into the old outer wall of ancient Rome's mammoth Theater of Pompey. Julius Caesar was assassinated in the Theater, where the Senate was meeting while its main Forum building was being repaired after a fire.

The square is surrounded by fun eateries, great for people-watching. Bruno faces the bustling Forno (in the left corner of the square, closed Sun), where takeout *pizza bianca* is sold hot out of the oven. On weekend nights, when the Campo is packed with beer-drinking kids, the medieval square is transformed into one vast Roman street party.

▶ *If Bruno did a hop, step, and jump forward, then turned right on Via dei Baullari and marched 200 yards, he'd cross the busy Corso Vittorio Emanuele; then, continuing another 150 yards on Via Cuccagna, he'd find...*

Piazza Navona

This long, oval piazza retains the oblong shape of the athletic grounds built here around A.D. 80 by the emperor Domitian. Since ancient times, the square has been a center of Roman life. In the 1800s, the city would flood the square to cool off the neighborhood.

The Four Rivers Fountain in the center is the most famous fountain by the man who remade Rome in Baroque style, Gian Lorenzo Bernini. Four burly river gods—representing the four quarters of the world—support an Egyptian-style obelisk. The water of the world gushes everywhere. The Nile has his head covered, since the headwaters were unknown then. The Ganges holds an oar. The Danube turns to admire the obelisk. And Uruguay's Río de la Plata tumbles backward in shock, wondering how he ever made the top four.

The Plata river god is gazing upward at the church of St. Agnes, worked on by Bernini's former student-turned-rival, Francesco Borromini. Borromini's concave facade helps reveal the dome and epitomizes the curved symmetry of Baroque. Tour guides say that Bernini designed his

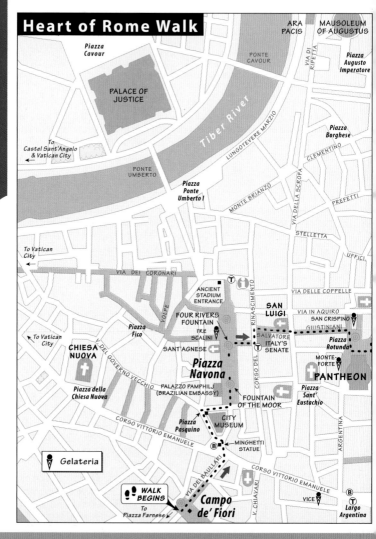

Heart of Rome Walk

- ARA PACIS
- MAUSOLEUM OF AUGUSTUS
- Piazza Cavour
- PONTE CAVOUR
- VIA DI RIPETTA
- Piazza Augusto Imperatore
- PALACE OF JUSTICE
- Tiber River
- To Castel Sant'Angelo & Vatican City
- LUNGOTEVERE MARZIO
- Piazza Borghese
- PONTE UMBERTO
- CLEMENTINO
- Piazza Ponte Umberto I
- MONTE BRIANZO
- VIA DELLA SCROFA
- PREFETTI
- To Vatican City
- VIA DEI CORONARI
- STELLETTA
- UFFICI
- VIA DELLE COPPELLE
- ANCIENT STADIUM ENTRANCE
- SAN LUIGI
- VIA IN AQUIRO
- RINASCIMENTO
- SAN CRISPINO
- GIUSTINIANI
- FOUR RIVERS FOUNTAIN
- TRE SCALINI
- Piazza Fico
- VOLPE
- To Vatican City
- SALVATORE
- ITALY'S SENATE
- Piazza Rotunda
- CHIESA NUOVA
- VIA DEL GOVERNO VECCHIO
- SANT'AGNESE
- Piazza Navona
- CORSO DEL
- MONTE FORTE
- PANTHEON
- Piazza della Chiesa Nuova
- PALAZZO PAMPHILJ (BRAZILIAN EMBASSY)
- FOUNTAIN OF THE MOOR
- Piazza Sant' Eustachio
- CORSO VITTORIO EMANUELE
- Piazza Pasquino
- CITY MUSEUM
- ARGENTINA
- MINGHETTI STATUE
- Gelateria
- B
- CORSO VITTORIO EMANUELE
- WALK BEGINS
- To Piazza Farnese
- VIA DEI BAULLARI
- Campo de' Fiori
- V. CHIAVARI
- VICE
- B
- T
- Largo Argentina

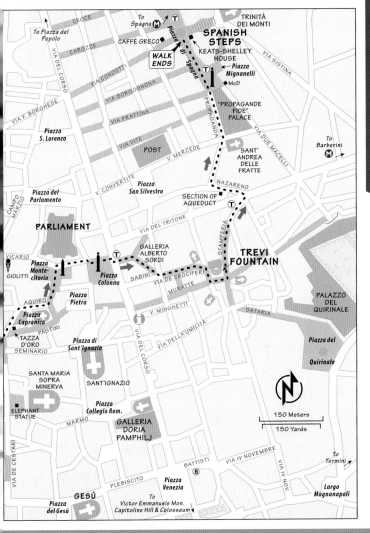

CROCE

To Piazza del Popolo

To Spagna (M) (T)

CAROZZE

VIA DEL CORSO

CAFFÈ GRECO

SPANISH STEPS

TRINITÀ DEI MONTI

KEATS-SHELLEY HOUSE

Piazza di Spagna

WALK ENDS

VIA CONDOTTI

VIA BORGOGNONA

VIA SISTINA

Piazza Mignanelli

McD

VIA FRATTINA

VIA F. BORGHESE

Piazza S. Lorenzo

VIA VITE

POST

PROPAGANDA

"PROPAGANDE FIDE" PALACE

To Barberini (M)

V. MERCEDE

VIA DUE MACELLI

SANT' ANDREA DELLE FRATTE

V. CONVERTITE

Piazza San Silvestro

SECTION OF AQUEDUCT

NAZARENO

CAMPO MARZIO

Piazza del Parlamento

VIA DEL TRITONE

(T)

STAMPERIA

PARLIAMENT

GALLERIA ALBERTO SORDI

TREVI FOUNTAIN

VICARIO

Piazza Montecitorio

(T)

GIOLITTI

Piazza Colonna

SABINI

VIA DE CROCIFERI

MURATTE

PALAZZO DEL QUIRINALE

AQUIRO

Piazza Pietra

PASTINI

V. MINGHETTI

DATARIA

Piazza Capranica

TAZZA D'ORO

Piazza del Quirinale

SEMINARIO

Piazza di Sant'Ignazio

VIA DELL'UMILITÀ

VIA DELL'UMILITÀ

SANTA MARIA SOPRA MINERVA

SANT'IGNAZIO

VIA DEL CORSO

ELEPHANT STATUE

Piazza Collegio Rom.

MARMO

N

GALLERIA DORIA PAMPHILJ

150 Meters

150 Yards

VIA DE CESTARI

BATTISTI

VIA IV NOVEMBRE

To Termini

GESÚ

PLEBISCITO

Piazza Venezia

(B)

VIA IV NOV.

Largo Magnanapoli

Piazza del Gesú

To Victor Emmanuele Mon. Capitoline Hill & Colosseum

Piazza Navona—fountains and nightlife

Bernini's Four Rivers Fountain

river god to look horrified at Borromini's work. Or maybe he's shielding his eyes from St. Agnes' nakedness, as she was stripped before being martyred. But either explanation is unlikely, since the fountain was completed two years before Borromini even started work on the church.

Piazza Navona is Rome's most interesting night scene, with street music, artists, fire-eaters, local Casanovas, ice cream, and outdoor cafés that are worthy of a splurge if you've got time to sit and enjoy Italy's human river.

▶ *Leave Piazza Navona directly across from Tre Scalini (famous for its rich chocolate gelato), and go east down Corsia Agonale, past rose peddlers and palm readers. Jog left around the guarded building (the Palazzo Madama, where Italy's senate meets), and follow the brown sign to the Pantheon, which is straight down Via del Salvatore.*

The Pantheon

Sit for a while under the floodlit and moonlit portico of the Pantheon.

The 40-foot, single-piece granite columns of the Pantheon's entrance show the scale the ancient Romans built on. The columns support a triangular Greek-style roof with an inscription that says "M. Agrippa" built it. In fact, it was built *(fecit)* by Emperor Hadrian (A.D. 120), who gave credit to the builder of an earlier structure. This impressive entranceway gives no clue that the greatest wonder of the building is inside—a domed room of perfect proportions that has inspired artists and architects through the ages. For more about the Pantheon's construction and interior, ✪ see page 132.

▶ *With your back to the Pantheon, veer to the right, uphill toward the yellow sign on Via Orfani that reads* Casa del Caffè *at the Tazza d'Oro coffee shop.*

The Pantheon—the temple to "all the gods"—is now the focus of all the tourists.

From the Pantheon to Piazza Colonna

Tazza d'Oro Casa del Caffè: One of Rome's top coffee shops, it dates back to the days when this area was licensed to roast coffee beans. Locals come here for its fine *granita di caffè con panna* (coffee slush with cream).

▶ *Continue up Via Orfani to...*

Piazza Capranica: This square is home to the big, plain Florentine Renaissance-style Palazzo Capranica (directly opposite as you enter the square). Big shots, like the Capranica family, built towers on their palaces—not for defense, but just to show off.

▶ *Leave the piazza to the right of the palace, heading down Via in Aquiro, which leads to the...*

Parliament: This well-guarded building is where Italy's lower house meets. You may see politicians, political demonstrations, and TV cameras. Out front is a sixth-century B.C. **Egyptian obelisk** taken as a trophy by Augustus after his victory in Egypt over Mark Antony and Cleopatra. The obelisk was set up as a sundial, with zodiac markings. Rome has 13 obelisks, more than any other city.

▶ *To your right is Piazza Colonna, where we're heading next—unless you like gelato...*

Giolitti's: A one-block detour to the left (past Albergo Nazionale) brings you to Rome's most famous *gelateria*. **Giolitti's** is cheap for take-out or elegant and splurge-worthy for a sit among classy locals (open daily until past midnight, Via Uffici del Vicario 40); get your gelato in a cone *(cono)* or cup *(coppetta)*.

Piazza Colonna features a huge second-century column. Its reliefs depict the victories of Emperor Marcus Aurelius over the barbarians. When Marcus died in A.D. 180, the barbarians began to get the upper hand, beginning Rome's long three-century fall. The big, important-looking palace houses the headquarters for the deputies (or cabinet) of the prime minister.

Via del Corso is Rome's main north-south boulevard, running ramrod-straight for a mile through the neighborhood's tangled streets. In ancient times, visitors from northern Europe entered along this road, where they got their first glimpse of the grand city. Via del Corso is named for the riderless horse races *(corse)* that took place here during Carnevale. In 1854, the Via became one of Rome's first gas-lit streets and hosted the classiest boutiques. Nowadays most of Via del Corso is closed to traffic for a few hours every evening and becomes a wonderful parade of Romans out for a stroll (✪ see page 144).

▶ *Cross Via del Corso to enter a big palatial building with columns, which houses the* **Galleria Alberto Sordi** *shopping mall. Inside, take the fork to the right and exit out the back. (If you're here after 21:00, when the mall is closed, circle around the right side of the Galleria on Via dei Sabini.) Once out the back, head up Via de Crociferi, to the roar of the water, lights, and people of...*

The Trevi Fountain

This watery Baroque avalanche celebrates the abundance of pure water, which has been brought into the city since the days of ancient aqueducts. Oceanus rides across the waves in his chariot, pulled by horses and horn-blowing tritons, as he commands the flow of water. The illustrious Bernini sketched out the first designs. Nicola Salvi continued the project (c. 1740), using the palace behind the fountain as a theatrical backdrop.

The scene is always lively, with lucky Romeos clutching dates while unlucky ones clutch beers. Take some time to people-watch and whisper a few breathy *bellos* or *bellas*.

Legend says if you throw a coin in, you'll be sure to return to Rome. Confused and creative types have expanded the legend—two coins brings romance, three means marriage (no coins means divorced and paying

The Trevi Fountain—make a wish, toss a coin, and dream.

alimony), coins must be thrown with the right hand over the left shoulder, etc. Hey, it's Rome by night and the world is yours—make your own wish.

▶ *From the Trevi Fountain, it's 10 minutes to our next stop, the Spanish Steps. Use a map to get there, or follow these directions: Facing the Trevi Fountain, go forward, walking along the right side of the fountain on Via della Stamperia. Cross the busy Via del Tritone. Continue 100 yards and veer right at Via delle Fratte, a street that changes its name to Via Propaganda before ending at...*

The Spanish Steps

The wide, curving staircase is one of Rome's iconic sights. Its 138 steps lead sharply up from Piazza di Spagna, forming a butterfly shape as they fan out around a central terrace. The design culminates at the top in an obelisk framed between two Baroque church towers.

Built in the 1720s by a little-known architect (Francesco de Sanctis), the steps are called "Spanish" because of the Spanish Embassy to the Vatican located here. In springtime, the already-picturesque staircase is often colored with flowers.

At the base of the steps is the playful "Sinking Boat" Barcaccia Fountain (1627-29), by Pietro Bernini and/or his famous son Gian Lorenzo. The half-submerged boat brims with water, recalling the urban legend of a fishing boat—supposedly lost during a 1598 flood of the Tiber—that ended up beached on this spot.

The Spanish Steps have been the hangout of many Romantics over the years (Keats, Wagner, Openshaw, Goethe, and others). The British poet John Keats pondered his mortality, and then died of tuberculosis (1821) at age 25 in the pink building on the right side of the steps. Fellow Romantic Lord Byron lived across the square at #66.

It's clear that the main sight here is not the steps but the people who gather around them. By day, shoppers swarm the high-fashion boutiques at the base of the steps, along Via Condotti. On warm evenings, the area is alive with young people in love with the city.

▶ *Our walk is finished. The Spagna Metro stop (usually open until 23:30, later on Fri-Sat) is to the left of the steps. Just outside the Metro is a WC (10:00-19:30) and a free elevator to the top of the steps (closes at 21:00). A huge McDonald's (with a WC) is a block to the right of the steps. When you're ready to leave, zip home on the Metro or grab a taxi at either end of the piazza.*

The Spanish Steps—less a historic monument than a gathering place for Rome today

Vatican Museums Tour

Musei Vaticani

The glories of the ancient world are on display in this lavish papal palace. Start with ancient Egyptian mummies and some of the best Greek and Roman statues in captivity. Then traverse long halls lined with old maps, tapestries, fig leaves, and broken penises. Pass through the popes' former home, where the painter Raphael boldly celebrated pagan philosophers in the heart of Christendom. Our visit culminates with Michelangelo's glorious Sistine Chapel, whose centerpiece shows God reaching out to pass the divine spark of life to man.

It's inspiring...and exhausting. But with this chapter as your guide, you'll easily sweep through 5,000 years of human history.

ORIENTATION

Cost: €17 plus €4 online reservation fee. Free on the last Sun of each month (when it's very crowded).

Hours: Mon-Sat 9:00-18:00, last entry at 16:00. Closed Sun, except last Sun of the month 9:00-14:00, last entry at 12:30. Open Fri nights mid April-Oct 19:00-23:00 (last entry at 21:30) by online reservation only. Guards start ushering people out of the museum 30 minutes before the official closing time. The museum is closed about a dozen days a year for religious holidays. Check the calendar and the latest hours for your exact visit the museum website.

Information: Tel. 06-6988-3860; www.museivaticani.va.

When to Go: The museum is generally hot and crowded, with waits of up to two hours to buy tickets and shoulder-to-shoulder crowds inside. The worst times are Saturdays, free Sundays, Mondays, rainy days, any day before or after a holiday closure, and mornings in general. Least crowded are late-afternoon weekdays.

Avoiding the Ticket-Buying Line: Bypass the long lines by reserving an entry time online (easy instructions, pay with credit card). Bring your reservation voucher to the Vatican Museums entrance, where you'll bypass the ticket-buying line and enter at the "Visitor Entrance with Online Reservations" line.

You can buy same-day, skip-the-line tickets from the TI on St. Peter's Square (to the left of the basilica), from a table in the portico of St. Peter's (with service fee tacked on), or by booking a guided tour (see below).

Dress Code: Modest dress is required (no short shorts or bare shoulders).

Getting There: Taxis take you right to the entrance—hop in and say, "moo-ZAY-ee vah-tee-KAH-nee." The Ottaviano Metro stop is a 10-minute walk from the entrance (❂ see map on page 146). Bus #64 stops on the other side of St. Peter's Square, a 20-minute walk away. Bus #492 (from the city center) is also handy. On foot from St. Peter's Square, face the church, take a right through the colonnade, and follow the Vatican Wall.

Tours: English tours are easy to book online (€32, includes admission) and allow you to skip the ticket line. Audioguides are €7. My free

🎧 Rick Steves audio tours cover the Vatican Museums and Sistine Chapel—◎ see page 195.

Length of This Tour: Until you expire, or 2.5 hours.

Security and Baggage Check: You pass through a metal detector (no pocket knives allowed). The baggage check (near security) takes only big bags, not day bags.

St. Peter's Shortcut: If you plan to visit St. Peter's Basilica right after the Vatican Museums, there's a shortcut that leads directly from the Sistine Chapel to St. Peter's Basilica (spilling out alongside the church; ◎ see map on page 46). This route saves you a 30-minute walk and lets you avoid the often-long security line at the basilica's main entrance. To take this shortcut, you'll need to: adhere to St. Peter's stricter dress code, drop off the Vatican Museums audioguide after leaving the Sistine Chapel, tour the Pinacoteca earlier, and be prepared for the odd chance that the shortcut may be closed (which sometimes happens).

Photography: No photos in the Sistine. Elsewhere, photos are OK without a flash.

Cuisine Art: A $ self-service cafeteria is inside (near the Pinacoteca), and smaller $$ cafés are in the Cortile della Pigna and near the Sistine Chapel. Outside the museum, there's cheap pizza by the slice along Viale Giulio Cesare. Picnickers can browse the colorful Mercato Trionfale produce market three blocks north of the entrance on Via Andrea Doria (head across the street, down the stairs, and continue straight). For restaurant recommendations, ◎ see page 175.

Starring: World history, from Egyptian mummies to Greek and Roman statues to Renaissance masters Raphael and Michelangelo.

THE TOUR BEGINS

This heavyweight museum is shaped like a barbell—two buildings connected by a long hall. The entrance building covers the ancient world (Egypt, Greece, Rome). The one at the far end covers its "rebirth" in the Renaissance (including the Sistine Chapel). The halls there and back are a mix of old and new. Move quickly—don't burn out before the Sistine

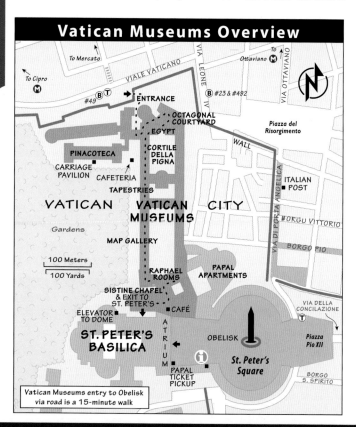

Vatican Museums Overview

To Mercato

To Cipro

VIALE VATICANO

VIA LEONE IV

To Ottaviano

VIA OTTAVIANO

#49 B T

ENTRANCE

B #23 & #492

OCTAGONAL COURTYARD

EGYPT

Piazza del Risorgimento

PINACOTECA

CORTILE DELLA PIGNA

WALL

CARRIAGE PAVILION

CAFETERIA

TAPESTRIES

ITALIAN POST

VATICAN

VATICAN MUSEUMS

CITY

Gardens

VIA DI PORTA ANGELICA

BORGO VITTORIO

BORGO PIO

MAP GALLERY

100 Meters
100 Yards

RAPHAEL ROOMS

PAPAL APARTMENTS

SISTINE CHAPEL & EXIT TO ST. PETER'S

CAFÉ

VIA DELLA CONCILIAZIONE

T

ELEVATOR TO DOME

ST. PETER'S BASILICA

A T R I U M

OBELISK

Piazza Pio XII

PAPAL TICKET PICKUP

St. Peter's Square

BORGO S. SPIRITO

Vatican Museums entry to Obelisk via road is a 15-minute walk

Chapel at the end—and see how each civilization borrows from and builds on the previous one.

▶ *Leave Italy by entering the doors.*

Once you clear the security checkpoint, exchange your printed voucher for a ticket (on the ground floor) or buy your ticket (upstairs). Scan the ticket in the turnstiles, then take the long escalator or spiral ramp up, up, up to a covered courtyard with a view of the St. Peter's dome. Pause at the courtyard: To your right is the cafeteria and the Pinacoteca painting gallery.

To start, go left, then take another left up a flight of stairs to reach the first-floor Egyptian Rooms (Museo Gregoriano Egizio) on your right. Don't stop until you find your mummy.

Note: If the stairs up to Egypt are temporarily closed off, just keep following the masses through the spacious Cortile della Pigna courtyard until you reach the Apollo Belvedere and Laocoön figures. Tour the museum from there to the "Sarcophagi," where you'll find the entrance to the Egyptian rooms.

EGYPT (3000-1000 B.C.)

Egyptian art was religious, not decorative. A statue or painting preserved the likeness of someone, giving him or her a form of eternal life. Most of the art was for tombs, where they put the mummies.

▶ *Pass beyond the imitation Egyptian pillars to the left of the case in the center of the room, and you'll find...*

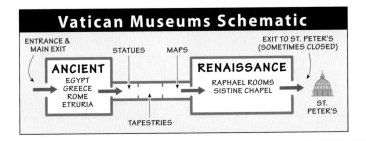

❶ Mummies

This woman died three millennia ago. Her corpse was disemboweled, and her organs were placed in a jar like those you see nearby. Then the body was refilled with pitch, dried with natron (a natural sodium carbonate), wrapped in linen, and placed in a wood coffin, which went inside a stone coffin, which was placed in a tomb. (Remember that the pyramids were just big tombs.) Notice the henna job on her hair—in the next life, your spirit needed a body to be rooted to...and you wanted to look your best.

Painted inside the coffin lid is a list of what the deceased "packed" for the journey to eternity. The coffins were decorated with magical spells to protect the body from evil and to act as crib notes for the confused soul in the netherworld.

▶ *In the next room are...*

❷ Egyptian Statues

Egyptian statues walk awkwardly, as if they're carrying heavy buckets, with arms straight down at their sides. Even these Roman reproductions (made for Hadrian's Villa) are stiff, two-dimensional, and schematic—the art is only realistic enough to get the job done. In Egyptian belief, a statue like this could be a stable refuge for the wandering soul of a dead man. Each was made according to an established set of proportions.

▶ *Walk through the next small room and into the curved hallway, with...*

❸ Egyptian Gods as Animals

Before technology made humans top dogs on earth, Egyptians saw the superiority of animals and worshipped them as incarnations of the gods. Wander through a pet store of Egyptian animal gods. Find Anubis, a jackal

Anubis—a jackal in a toga

Sumerian writing on clay tablets

in a toga. In the curved room, find the lioness, the fierce goddess Sekhmet. The clever baboon is the god of wisdom, Thoth. At the end of the curved hall on your right is Bes (the small white marble statue), the patron of pregnant women (and beer-bellied men).

▶ *Continue to Room VIII (the third room), pausing at the glass case, which contains brown clay tablets.*

❹ Sumerian Writing
Even before Egypt, civilizations flourished in the Middle East. The Sumerian culture in Mesopotamia (the ancestors of the ancient Babylonians and today's Iraqis) invented writing in about 3000 B.C. People wrote on clay tablets by pressing into the wet clay with a wedge-shaped (cuneiform) pen. The Sumerians also rolled cylindrical seals into soft clay to make an impression used to authenticate documents and mark property.

▶ *Pass through the next room, and then turn left, to a balcony with a view of Rome through the window. Then enter the octagonal courtyard.*

SCULPTURE—GREECE AND ROME (500 B.C.-A.D. 500)

This palace wouldn't be here, this sculpture wouldn't be here, and our lives would likely be quite different if it weren't for a few thousand Greeks in a small city about 450 years before Christ. Athens set the tone for the rest of the West. Democracy, theater, economics, literature, and art all flourished in Athens during a 50-year "Golden Age." Greek culture was then appropriated by Rome, and revived again 1,500 years later, during the Renaissance. The Renaissance popes built and decorated these papal palaces, re-creating the glory of the classical world.

❺ Apollo Belvedere
Apollo, the god of the sun and of music, is hunting. He's been running through the woods, and now he spots his prey. Keeping his eye on the animal, he slows down and prepares to put a (missing) arrow into his (missing) bow. The optimistic Greeks conceived of their gods in human form... and buck naked.

This Roman copy of a Hellenistic original followed the style of the greater Greek sculptor Praxiteles, and fully captured the beauty of the human form. The anatomy is perfect, his pose is natural. Instead of standing

Apollo Belvedere—a god in human form

"Snakes! Why did it have to be snakes?"

at attention, face-forward with his arms at his sides (Egyptian-style), Apollo is on the move, coming to rest, with his weight on one leg.

The Greeks loved balance. A well-rounded man was both a thinker and an athlete, a poet and a warrior. In art, the Apollo Belvedere balances several opposites. He's moving, but not out of control. Apollo eyes his target, but hasn't attacked yet. He's realistic, but with idealized, godlike features. The only sour note: his left hand, added in modern times. Could we try a size smaller?

▶ *In the neighboring niche to the right, a bearded old Roman river god lounges in the shade. This pose inspired Michelangelo's Adam, in the Sistine Chapel (coming up soon).*

⑥ Laocoön

Laocoön (lay-AWK-oh-wahn), the high priest of Troy, warned his fellow Trojans: "Beware of Greeks bearing gifts." The attacking Greeks had brought the Trojan Horse to the gates as a ploy to get inside the city walls, and Laocoön tried to warn his people not to bring it inside. But the gods wanted the Greeks to win, so they sent huge snakes to crush Laocoön and his two sons to death. We see them at the height of their terror, when they realize that, no matter how hard they struggle, they—and their entire race—are doomed.

The figures (carved from four blocks of marble pieced together seamlessly) are powerful, not light and graceful. The poses are as twisted as possible, accentuating every rippling muscle and bulging vein. Follow the line of motion from Laocoön's left foot, up his leg, through his body, and out his right arm (which some historians used to think extended straight

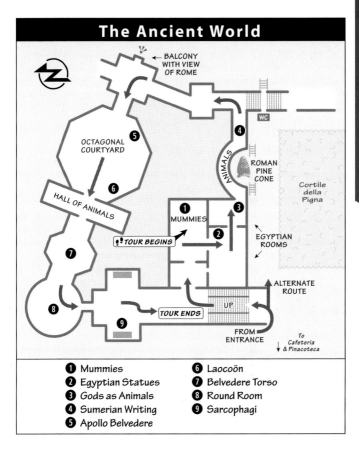

The Ancient World

← BALCONY
WITH VIEW
OF ROME

WC

5 OCTAGONAL COURTYARD

ROMAN
PINE
CONE

Cortile
della
Pigna

6 HALL OF ANIMALS

4

ANIMALS

1 MUMMIES

3

2

! TOUR BEGINS

EGYPTIAN
ROOMS

7

ALTERNATE
ROUTE

8

9

TOUR ENDS

UP

FROM
ENTRANCE

To
Cafeteria
& Pinacoteca

1 Mummies
2 Egyptian Statues
3 Gods as Animals
4 Sumerian Writing
5 Apollo Belvedere
6 Laocoön
7 Belvedere Torso
8 Round Room
9 Sarcophagi

out—until the elbow was dug up early in the 1900s). Goethe would stand here and blink his eyes rapidly, watching the statue flicker to life.

Laocoön was sculpted some four centuries after the Golden Age, after the scales of "balance" had been tipped. Whereas Apollo is poised, graceful, and godlike, Laocoön is restless, emotional, and gritty.

Laocoön—the most famous Greek statue in ancient Rome—was lost for more than a thousand years. Then, in 1506, it was unexpectedly un-earthed near the Colosseum. They cleaned it off and paraded it through the streets before an awestruck populace. Young Michelangelo saw the statue; its unbridled motion influenced his work in the Sistine Chapel, which itself influenced generations of artists.

▶ *Leave the courtyard to the right of Laocoön and swing around the Hall of Animals, a jungle of beasts real and surreal. Then continue to the limbless torso in the middle of the next large hall.*

⑦ Belvedere Torso

This rough hunk of shaped rock makes you appreciate the sheer physical labor involved in chipping a figure out of solid stone. It takes great strength, but at the same time, great delicacy.

This is all that remains of an ancient statue of Hercules seated on a lion skin. Michelangelo loved this old rock. As the best sculptor of his day, his only peers were the ancients. He'd caress this statue lovingly and say, "I am the pupil of the Torso." To him, it contained all the beauty of classical sculpture, though compared with the pure grace of the *Apollo*, it's down-right ugly.

Michelangelo, an ugly man himself, wasn't looking for the beauty of idealized gods, but the innate beauty of every person, even so-called ugly ones. With its knotty lumps of muscle, the Torso has a brute power and a distinct personality despite—or because of—its rough edges.

▶ *Enter the next, domed room.*

⑧ Round Room

This room, modeled on the Pantheon interior, gives some idea of Roman

Belvedere Torso—ugly beauty

Hercules—Roman grandeur

grandeur. Romans took Greek ideas and made them bigger, like the big bronze statue of Hercules with his club. The mosaic floor once decorated the bottom of a pool in an ancient Roman bath. The enormous Roman basin/hot tub/birdbath/vase, which once decorated Nero's palace, is made of a single block of purple porphyry marble imported from Egypt. Purple was the color of emperors, and—since porphyry doesn't occur naturally in Italy—it was also rare and expensive.

▶ *Enter the next room. The two large purple* **9** ***Sarcophagi*** *were made (though not used) for the Roman emperor Constantine's mother and daughter.*

   See how we've come full circle in this building—the Egyptian Rooms are ahead on your left. Go upstairs and begin the Long March down the hall lined with statues (the Gallery of the Candelabra) leading to the Sistine Chapel and Raphael Rooms.

THE LONG MARCH—
SCULPTURE, TAPESTRIES, MAPS, AND VIEWS

This quarter-mile walk gives you a sense of the grandeur of the former papal palaces, once decorated with statues, urns, marble floors, friezes, tapestries, and stuccoed ceilings. As heirs of imperial Rome, the popes of the Renaissance felt they deserved such luxury. It was their extravagant spending on palaces like this that inspired Martin Luther to rebel, starting the Protestant Reformation.

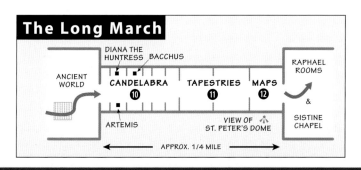

The Long March

DIANA THE HUNTRESS   BACCHUS

ANCIENT WORLD

CANDELABRA **10**

TAPESTRIES **11**

MAPS **12**

RAPHAEL ROOMS

&

ARTEMIS

VIEW OF ST. PETER'S DOME

SISTINE CHAPEL

◀——— APPROX. 1/4 MILE ———▶

Artemis—Boobs or bulls' balls?

Tapestry that "moves" as you pass

⑩ Gallery of the Candelabra: Classical Sculpture

In the second "room" of the long hall, stop at the statue (on the left) of **Diana,** the virgin goddess of the hunt. Roman hunters would pray and give offerings to statues like this to get divine help in their search for food.

Farmers might pray to another version of the same goddess, **Artemis,** on the opposite wall. "Boobs or bulls' balls?" Some historians say this billion-breasted beauty stood for fertility. Others contend that bulls were sacrificed and castrated, with the testicles draped over the statues as symbols of fertility.

Shuffle along to the next "room," where (on the left) is a statue of **Bacchus,** with a baby on his shoulders. Like many classical statues, Bacchus may have originally been painted—brown hair, rosy cheeks, purple grapes, and a leopard-skin sidekick at his feet. Also, many statues had glass eyes like Bacchus.

And the fig leaves? Those came from the years 1550 to 1800, when the Church decided that certain parts of the human anatomy were obscene. (Why not the feet?) Perhaps Church leaders associated these full-frontal statues with the outbreak of Renaissance humanism that reduced their power in Europe. Whatever the cause, they reacted by covering classical crotches with plaster fig leaves, the same leaves Adam and Eve had used when the concept of "privates" was invented.

▶ *Cover your eyes in case they forgot a fig leaf or two, and continue to the tapestries.*

⑪ Tapestries

Along the left wall are tapestries designed by Raphael's workshop and made in Brussels. They show scenes from the life of Christ: Baby Jesus in the manger, being adored by shepherds, and presented in the temple. *The Supper at Emmaus* tapestry (with Jesus sitting at a table) is curiously interactive. As you walk, the end of the table seems to follow you.

On the ceiling, admire the workmanship of the sculpted reliefs, then realize that it's not a relief at all—it's painted on a flat surface.

⑫ Map Gallery and View of Vatican City

This gallery—crusted with a ceiling of colorful stucco and lined with colorful maps—still feels like a pope's palace. The maps (16th-century) let popes take visitors on a virtual tour of Italy's regions, from the toe (entrance end) to the Alps (far end). The scenes on the ceiling portray exciting moments in Church history in each of those regions.

Glance out the windows at the tiny country of Vatican City, established in 1929. It has its own radio station, as you see from the tower on the hill. What you see here is pretty much all there is—these gardens, the palaces you're in, and St. Peter's (lean out and look left for a good view of Michelangelo's dome).

▶ *Exit the map room and take a breather. When you're ready, rejoin the flow and turn left, on the route leading to the Raphael Rooms.*

The Map Gallery gives a glimpse of the former luxury of the palace of the popes.

RENAISSANCE ART

Raphael Rooms: Papal Wallpaper

We've seen art from the ancient world; now we'll see its rebirth in the Renaissance. We're entering the living quarters of the great Renaissance popes—where they slept, worked, and worshipped. They hired the best artists—mostly from Florence—to paint the walls and ceilings, combining classical and Christian motifs.

Entering, you'll immediately see a huge (non-Raphael) painting that depicts the ⑬ **Polish King Jan III Sobieski** liberating Vienna from the Ottomans in 1683, finally tipping the tide in favor of a Christian Europe.

The second room's (non-Raphael) paintings celebrate the doctrine of the ⑭ **Immaculate Conception,** establishing that Mary herself was born without sin. The largest fresco shows how the inspiration came straight from heaven (upper left) in a thin ray of light directly to the pope.

▶ *Next, you'll pass along an outside walkway that overlooks a courtyard (is that the pope's Fiat?), finally ending up in the first of the Raphael Rooms, the...*

⑮ Constantine Room

The frescoes (which were finished by Raphael's assistants, notably Giulio Romano) celebrate the passing of the baton from pagan Rome to Christian Rome. On the night of October 27, A.D. 312 (left wall), as General Constantine (in gold, with crown) was preparing his troops for a coup d'état, he looked up. He saw a cross in the sky with the words, "You will conquer in this sign."

The next day (long wall), his troops raged into battle with the Christian cross atop their Roman eagle banners. There's Constantine in the center with a smile on his face, slashing through the enemy, while God's warrior angels ride shotgun overhead.

Victorious, Constantine stripped (right wall) and knelt before the pope to be baptized a Christian (some say). As emperor, he legalized Christianity and worked hand-in-hand with the pope (window wall). When Rome fell, its glory lived on through the Dark Ages in the pomp, pageantry, and learning of the Catholic Church.

Look at the ceiling painting. A classical statue is knocked backward, crumbling before the overpowering force of the cross. Whoa! Christianity

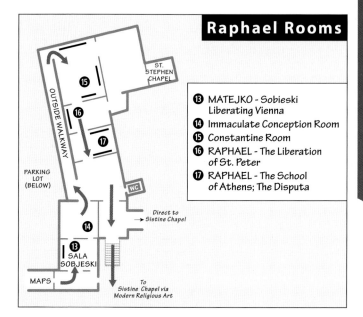

Raphael Rooms

- **13** MATEJKO - Sobieski Liberating Vienna
- **14** Immaculate Conception Room
- **15** Constantine Room
- **16** RAPHAEL - The Liberation of St. Peter
- **17** RAPHAEL - The School of Athens; The Disputa

triumphs over pagan Rome. (This was painted, I believe, by Raphael's sur-realist colleague, Salvadorus Dalio.)

▶ *While viewing these frescoes, ponder the life and times of...*

Raphael

Raphael was only 25 when Pope Julius II—the same man who hired Michelangelo to paint the Sistine Ceiling—invited him to paint the walls of his personal living quarters.

Raphael lived a charmed life. He was handsome and sophisticated, and painted masterpieces effortlessly. In a different decade, he might have been thrown out of the Church as a great sinner, but his love affairs and devil-may-care personality seemed to epitomize the optimistic pagan spirit of the Renaissance. His works are graceful but never lightweight or frilly—they're realistic, balanced, and harmonious. When he died young in 1520, the High Renaissance died with him.

▶ *Continue on. In a room or two (depending on the current route), you'll reach a room with frescoes arching over the windows, including Raphael's* ⓰ **The Liberation of St. Peter.** *It shows Peter, Jesus' right-hand man, being rescued from prison by a bright angel. In the next room—the pope's private study—Raphael painted...*

⓱ *The School of Athens*

In both style and subject matter, this fresco sums up the spirit of the Renaissance—the rebirth of classical art, literature, and science, and the optimistic spirit that man is a rational creature. Raphael pays respect to the great thinkers of ancient Greece, gathering them together at one time in a mythical school setting.

In the center are Plato and Aristotle, the two greatest Greeks. Plato points up, indicating his philosophy that mathematics and pure ideas are the source of truth, while Aristotle points down, showing preference for hands-on study of the material world. There's their master, Socrates (midway to the left, in green), ticking off arguments on his fingers. And in the foreground at right, bald Euclid bends over a slate to demonstrate a geometrical formula.

The School of Athens—ancient philosophers with contemporary faces, including Michelangelo's

Raphael shows that Renaissance thinkers were as good as the ancients. There's Leonardo da Vinci, whom Raphael worshipped, in the role of Plato. Euclid is the architect Donato Bramante, who designed St. Peter's. Raphael himself (next to last on the far right, with the black beret) looks out at us. And the "school" building is actually an early version of St. Peter's Basilica, under construction at the time.

Raphael balances everything symmetrically—thinkers to the left, scientists to the right, with Plato and Aristotle dead center—showing the geometrical order found in the world. Look at the square floor tiles in the foreground. If you laid a ruler over them and extended the line upward, it would run right to the center of the picture. Similarly, the tops of the columns all point down to the middle. All the lines of sight draw our attention to Plato and Aristotle, and to the small arch over their heads—a halo over these two secular saints in the divine pursuit of knowledge.

While Raphael was putting the finishing touches on this room, Michelangelo was at work down the hall in the Sistine Chapel. Raphael got a peek at Michelangelo's powerful work, and was astonished. He returned to *The School of Athens* and added one more figure to the scene—Michelangelo, the brooding, melancholy figure in front, leaning on a block of marble.

On the opposite wall, Raphael's **La Disputa** portrays how grace descends from Christ (at top) via the Holy Spirit (the dove, in the center) into the Communion wafer (on the altar below).

▶ *Pause here and plan. (WCs are nearby, but sometimes closed.) Leaving the Raphael Rooms, you could turn left to go directly to the Sistine. Or...*

Bearing right (a five-minute walk and a few staircases longer) gets you to the Sistine by way of the impressive Modern Religious Art collection. Though longer, this route leads to quiet rooms at the foot of the stairs, with benches where you can sit in peace and read ahead before entering the hectic Sistine Chapel. Your call.

THE SISTINE CHAPEL

The Sistine Chapel contains Michelangelo's ceiling and his huge *The Last Judgment*. The Sistine is the personal chapel of the pope and the place where new popes are elected.

When Pope Julius II asked Michelangelo to take on this important project, he said, *"No, grazie."* Michelangelo insisted he was a sculptor, not a painter. The Sistine ceiling was a vast undertaking, and he didn't want to do a half-vast job. But the pope pleaded, bribed, and threatened until Michelangelo finally consented, on the condition that he be able to do it all his own way.

Julius had asked for only 12 apostles along the sides of the ceiling, but Michelangelo had a grander vision—the entire history of the world until Jesus. He spent the next four years (1508-1512) craning his neck on scaffolding six stories up, covering the ceiling with frescoes of biblical scenes.

In sheer physical terms, it's an astonishing achievement: 5,900 square feet, with the vast majority done by his own hand. (Raphael only designed most of his rooms, letting assistants do the grunt work.)

First, he had to design and erect the scaffolding. Any materials had to be hauled up on pulleys. Then, a section of ceiling would be plastered. With fresco—painting on wet plaster—if you don't get it right the first time, you have to scrape the whole thing off and start over. And if you've ever struggled with a ceiling light fixture or worked under a car for even five minutes, you know how heavy your arms get. The physical effort, the paint dripping in his eyes, the creative drain, and the mental stress from a pushy pope combined to almost kill Michelangelo.

But when the ceiling was finished and revealed to the public, it simply blew 'em away. Like the *Laocoön* statue discovered six years earlier, it was unlike anything seen before. It both caps the Renaissance and turns it in a new direction. In perfect Renaissance spirit, it mixes Old Testament prophets with classical figures. But the style is more dramatic, shocking, and emotional than the balanced Renaissance works before it. This is a very personal work—the Gospel according to Michelangelo—but its themes and subject matter are universal. Many art scholars contend that the Sistine ceiling is the single greatest work of art by any one human being.

The Sistine Schematic

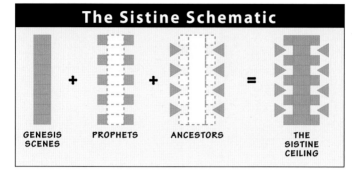

GENESIS SCENES + **PROPHETS** + **ANCESTORS** = **THE SISTINE CEILING**

The Sistine Ceiling: Understanding What You're Standing Under

The ceiling shows the history of the world before the birth of Jesus. We see God creating the world, creating man and woman, destroying the earth by flood, and so on. God himself, in his purple robe, actually appears in the first five scenes. Along the sides (where the ceiling starts to curve), we see the Old Testament prophets and pagan Greek prophetesses who foretold the coming of Christ. Dividing these scenes and figures are fake niches (a painted 3-D illusion) decorated with nude statue-like figures with symbolic meaning.

The key is to see three simple divisions in the tangle of bodies:

1. The central spine of nine rectangular biblical scenes;
2. The line of prophets on either side; and
3. The triangles between the prophets showing the ancestors of Christ.

▶ *Within the chapel, grab a seat along the side (if there's room). Face the altar with the big* **The Last Judgment** *on the wall (more on that later). Now look up to the ceiling and find the central panel of...*

The Creation of Adam

God and man take center stage in this Renaissance version of creation. Adam, newly formed in the image of God, lounges dreamily in perfect naked innocence. God, with his entourage, swoops in with a swirl of activity (which—with a little imagination—looks like a cross-section of a human brain...quite a strong humanist statement). Their reaching hands are the center of this work. Adam's is limp and passive; God's is strong and

The Sistine Ceiling

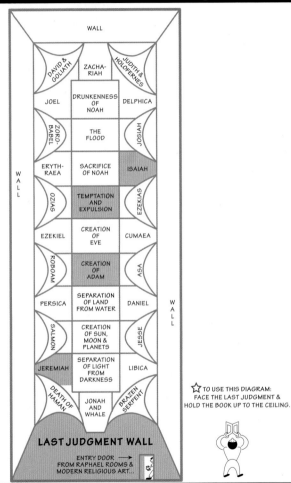

WALL

DAVID & GOLIATH

ZACHA-RIAH

JUDITH & HOLOFERNES

JOEL

DRUNKENNESS OF NOAH

DELPHICA

ZORO-BABEL

THE FLOOD

JOSIAH

ERYTH-RAEA

SACRIFICE OF NOAH

ISAIAH

OZIAS

TEMPTATION AND EXPULSION

EZEKIAS

EZEKIEL

CREATION OF EVE

CUMAEA

ROBOAM

CREATION OF ADAM

ASA

PERSICA

SEPARATION OF LAND FROM WATER

DANIEL

SALMON

CREATION OF SUN, MOON & PLANETS

JESSE

JEREMIAH

SEPARATION OF LIGHT FROM DARKNESS

LIBICA

DEATH OF HAMAN

JONAH AND WHALE

BRAZEN SERPENT

WALL

WALL

☆ TO USE THIS DIAGRAM:
FACE THE LAST JUDGMENT &
HOLD THE BOOK UP TO THE CEILING.

LAST JUDGMENT WALL

ENTRY DOOR →
FROM RAPHAEL ROOMS &
MODERN RELIGIOUS ART...

The Creation of Adam—God and man exchange meaningful eye contact, almost like equals

forceful, his finger twitching upward with energy. Here is the very moment of creation, as God passes the spark of life to man, the crowning work of his creation.

This is the spirit of the Renaissance. God is not a terrifying giant reaching down to puny and helpless man from way on high. Here they are on an equal plane, divided only by the diagonal patch of sky. God's billowing robe and the patch of green upon which Adam is lying balance each other. They are like two pieces of a jigsaw puzzle, or two long-separated continents, or like the yin and yang symbols finally coming together—uniting, complementing each other, creating wholeness. God and man work together in the divine process of creation.

▶ *This celebration of man permeates the ceiling. Notice the Adonises-come-to-life on the pedestals that divide the central panels. And then came woman.*

The Garden of Eden: Temptation and Expulsion

In one panel, we see two scenes from the Garden of Eden. On the left is the leafy garden of paradise where Adam and Eve lie around blissfully. But the devil comes along—a serpent with a woman's torso—and winds around the forbidden Tree of Knowledge. The temptation to gain new knowledge is too great for these Renaissance people. They eat the forbidden fruit.

At right, the sword-wielding angel drives them from Paradise into the barren plains. They're grieving, but they're far from helpless. Adam's body is thick and sturdy, and we know they'll survive in the cruel world. Adam firmly gestures to the angel, like he's saying, "All right, already! We're going!"

The Nine Scenes from Genesis

Take some time with these central scenes to understand the story that the ceiling tells. They run in sequence, starting at the front:

1. God, in purple, divides the light from darkness.
2. God creates the sun (burning orange) and the moon (pale white, to the right). Oops, I guess there's another moon.
3. God bursts toward us to separate the land and water.
4. God creates Adam.
5. God creates Eve, who dives into existence out of Adam's side.
6. Adam and Eve are tempted, then expelled, from the Garden of Eden.
7. Noah kills a ram and stokes the altar fires to make a sacrifice to God.
8. The great flood, sent by God, destroys the wicked, who desperately head for higher ground. In the distance, the ark carries Noah's family to safety. The blank spot dates to 1793, when a nearby gunpowder depot exploded, shaking the plaster loose.
9. Noah's sons see their drunken father. Perhaps Michelangelo chose to end his work with this scene as a reminder that even the best of men are fallible.

Prophets

You'll notice that the figures at the far end of the chapel are a bit smaller than those over *The Last Judgment.*

Michelangelo started at the far end, with the Noah scenes. By 1510, he'd finished the first half of the ceiling. When they took the scaffolding down and could finally see what he'd been working on for two years,

Prophet Isaiah—stately

Prophet Jeremiah—brooding

everyone was awestruck—except Michelangelo. As powerful as his figures are, from the floor they didn't look dramatic enough for Michelangelo. For the other half, he pulled out all the stops.

Compare the Noah scenes (far end) with their many small figures to the huge images of God at the other end. Similarly, Isaiah (near the lattice screen, marked "Esaias") is stately and balanced, while Jeremiah ("Hieremias," in the corner by *The Last Judgment*) is a dark, brooding figure. This prophet who witnessed the destruction of Israel slumps his chin in his hand and ponders the fate of his people. Like the difference between the stately Apollo Belvedere and the excited Laocoön, Michelangelo added a new emotional dimension to Renaissance painting.

▶ *The huge fresco on the altar wall (❂ pictured on page 78) is...*

The Last Judgment

When Michelangelo returned to paint the altar wall 23 years later (1535), the mood of Europe—and of the artist—was completely different. The Protestant Reformation had forced the Catholic Church to clamp down on free thought, and religious wars raged. Rome had recently been pillaged by roving bands of mercenaries. The Renaissance spirit of optimism was fading. Michelangelo himself had begun to question the innate goodness of mankind.

It's Judgment Day, and Christ—the powerful figure in the center, raising his arm to spank the wicked—has come to find out who's naughty and who's nice. Beneath him, a band of angels blows its trumpets Dizzy Gillespie-style, giving a wake-up call to the sleeping dead. The dead at lower left leave their graves and prepare to be judged. The righteous, on Christ's right hand (the left side of the picture), are carried up to the glories of heaven. The wicked on the other side are hurled down to hell, where demons wait to torture them. Charon, from the underworld of Greek mythology, waits below to ferry the souls of the damned to hell.

It's a grim picture. No one, but no one, is smiling. Even many of the righteous being resurrected (lower left) are either skeletons or cadavers with ghastly skin. The angels have to play tug-of-war with subterranean monsters to drag them from their graves.

Over in hell, the wicked are tortured by gleeful demons. One of the damned (to the right of the trumpeting angels) has an utterly lost expression, as if saying, "Why did I cheat on my wife?!" Two demons grab him around the ankles to pull him down to the bowels of hell, condemned to an eternity of constipation.

But it's the terrifying figure of Christ that dominates this scene. He raises his arm to smite the wicked, sending a ripple of fear through everyone. Even Mary beneath his arm (whose interceding days are clearly over) shrinks back in terror at loving Jesus' uncharacteristic outburst. His expression is completely closed, and he turns his head, refusing to even listen to the whining alibis of the damned. Look at Christ's twisting upper body. If this muscular figure looks familiar to you, it's because you've seen it before—the Belvedere Torso.

When *The Last Judgment* was unveiled to the public in 1541, it caused a sensation. The pope is said to have dropped to his knees and cried, "Lord, charge me not with my sins when thou shalt come on the Day of Judgment."

And it changed the course of art. The complex composition, with more than 300 figures swirling around the figure of Christ, went far beyond traditional Renaissance balance. The twisted figures shown from every imaginable angle challenged other painters to try and top this master of 3-D illusion. And the sheer terror and drama of the scene was a striking contrast to the placid optimism of, say, Raphael's *School of Athens*. Michelangelo had Baroque-en all the rules of the Renaissance, signaling a new era of art.

With the Renaissance fading, the fleshy figures in *The Last Judgment* aroused murmurs of discontent from Church authorities. (After Michelangelo's death, prudish Church authorities painted many of the wisps of clothing that we see today.) Michelangelo rebelled by painting his chief critic into the scene—in hell. He's the jackassed demon in the bottom right corner, wrapped in a snake. Look at how Michelangelo covered his privates. Sweet revenge.

If *The Creation of Adam* was the epitome of the optimistic Renaissance, *The Last Judgment* marks its end. Michelangelo himself must have wondered how he would be judged—had he used his God-given talents wisely? Look at St. Bartholomew, the bald, bearded guy at Christ's left foot (our right). In the flayed skin he's holding is a barely recognizable face—the twisted self-portrait of a self-questioning Michelangelo.

► *There are two exits from the Sistine Chapel. To return to the main entrance/exit and the Pinacoteca (a 15-minute walk away), leave the Sistine through the side door next to the screen.*

Or, if you're planning to take the shortcut directly to St. Peter's Basilica (*see map on page 56), exit out the far-right corner of the Sistine Chapel (with your back to the altar). Though this corner door is likely labeled "Exit for private tour groups only," you can usually just slide through with the crowds (or protest that your group has left you behind). If for some reason this exit is closed, hang out in the Sistine Chapel for a few more minutes—it'll likely reopen shortly.*

The Last Judgment

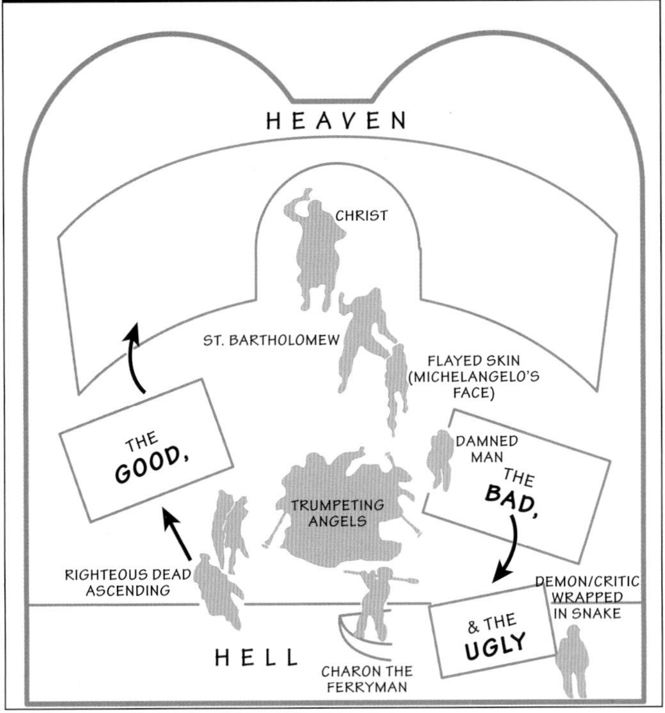

HEAVEN

CHRIST

ST. BARTHOLOMEW

FLAYED SKIN
(MICHELANGELO'S
FACE)

THE
GOOD,

DAMNED
MAN
THE
BAD,

TRUMPETING
ANGELS

RIGHTEOUS DEAD
ASCENDING

DEMON/CRITIC
WRAPPED
IN SNAKE

& THE
UGLY

HELL   CHARON THE
FERRYMAN

The Long March Back

Along this corridor (located one floor below the long corridor that you walked to get here), you'll see some of the wealth amassed by the popes, mostly gifts from royalty. Find your hometown on the 1529 map of the world: Look in the land labeled *"Terra Incognita."* The elaborately decorated library that branches off to the right contains rare manuscripts.

▸ *The corridor eventually spills out back outside. If you still have energy, follow signs to the...*

PINACOTECA

Like Lou Gehrig batting behind Babe Ruth, the Pinacoteca (Painting Gallery) has to follow the mighty Sistine & Co. But it offers a time-lapse walk through the art from medieval to Baroque with just a few stops.

Melozzo da Forli, *Musician Angels* (Room IV): These playful and delicate frescoes show heavenly musicians in soothing primary colors, even light, and classical purity. Rock on.

Raphael, *The Transfiguration* (Room VIII): Christ floats above a stumpy mountaintop, visited in a vision by the prophets Moses and Elijah. His disciples cower in awe as their savior is transfigured before them. Before Raphael died in 1520 (at age 37), the last thing he painted was the beatific face of Jesus, perhaps the most beautiful Christ in existence. When Raphael was buried in the Pantheon, this work accompanied the funeral.

Leonardo da Vinci, *St. Jerome*, c. 1482 (Room IX): Jerome squats in the rocky desert. He's spent too much time alone, fasting and meditating on his sins. His soulful face is echoed by his friend, the roaring lion. Though unfinished, this painting by Leonardo packs a psychological punch. Jerome's emaciated body expresses his intense penitence, while his pleading eyes hold a glimmer of hope for forgiveness. Leonardo wrote that a good painter must paint two things: "man and the movements of his spirit."

Caravaggio, *Deposition*, c. 1604 (Room XII): Christ is being buried. In the dark tomb, the faces of his followers emerge, lit by a harsh light. Christ's body has a deathlike color. We see Christ's dirty toes and Nicodemus' wrinkled, sunburned face. A tangle of grief looms out of the darkness as Christ's heavy, dead body nearly pulls the whole group with him from the cross into the tomb. After this museum, I know how he feels.

Musician Angels, by Melozzo

The Transfiguration, by Raphael

St. Peter's Basilica Tour

Basilica San Pietro

St. Peter's is the greatest church in Christendom. Its vast expanse could swallow up other churches whole. The basilica represents the power and splendor of Rome's 2,000-year domination of the Western world. Built on the memory and grave of the first pope, St. Peter, this is where the grandeur of ancient Rome became the grandeur of Christianity.

Besides sheer size, St. Peter's houses Michelangelo's dreamy *Pietà* and Bernini's towering bronze canopy. It's the place where the pope presides, and we'll catch a glimpse of the papal apartments nearby. We'll finish our visit with a sweaty climb up Michelangelo's dome for a one-of-a-kind view of Rome.

ORIENTATION

Cost: Free entry to basilica and crypt. Dome climb-€8 to climb stairs up, €10 to take an elevator for part of the climb. Treasury Museum-€7.

Dress Code: No shorts, above-the-knee skirts, or bare shoulders. This dress code is strictly enforced. Bring a cover-up, if necessary.

Hours of Church: Daily April-Sept 7:00-19:00, Oct-March 7:00-18:30. The church closes Wednesday mornings during papal audiences. Mass is held almost hourly every day, generally in the south (left) transept. Confirm the schedule on-site or at www.vatican.va. The Treasury Museum is open daily 8:00-18:50, Oct-March until 17:50. The Crypt is daily 9:00-16:00.

Dome Climb (Cupola): Daily from 8:00; if you're climbing the stairs all the way up, the last entry time is 17:00 (16:00 Oct-March). You take the elevator or stairs to roof level (with good views), then continue up stairs to the top of the dome (stunning views). The entrance (follow signs to the *cupola*) is just outside the basilica on the north side of St. Peter's (though the line often backs up to the church's front steps).

Getting There: From Metro stop Ottaviano, it's a 10-minute walk. Bus #40 stops at Piazza Pio, next to Castel Sant'Angelo—a 10-minute walk. Bus #64 stops just south of St. Peter's Square. (After crossing the Tiber, get off at the first stop past the tunnel; backtrack toward the tunnel and turn left when you see the columns of St. Peter's Square.) A taxi from Termini train station costs about €13. For a map of the Vatican area, ✪ see page 146.

Avoiding the Line: To bypass the long security-checkpoint line, consider visiting the Vatican Museums first, then taking the shortcut from the Sistine Chapel directly to St. Peter's (✪ get details on page 55 and see map on page 46).

Avoiding Crowds: The best time to visit the church is before 10:00. After 16:00 is also less crowded (and there's a music-filled Mass at 17:00), but the altar area is roped off to sightseers. The church is especially crowded on days when the pope makes appearances.

Information: The TI on the left (south) side of the square is excellent (Mon-Sat 8:30-18:15). Tel. 06-6988-1662, www.vaticanstate.va.

Services: WCs are on both sides of St. Peter's Square (by the TI and just outside security), near the baggage checkroom, and on the roof. The

Vatican City post office, next to the TI (Mon-Sat 8:30-18:30, closed Sun), sells postcards and its famous stamps (postboxes nearby).

Tours: Free 1.5-hour tours depart from the TI, generally Mon-Fri at 14:15 (confirm schedule at TI, tel. 06-6988-1662).

Audioguides are €5 plus ID. Or ⌖ download my free Rick Steves audio tour of the basilica (✪ see page 195).

Seeing the Pope: Your best bets are on Sundays and Wednesdays. To find out the pope's schedule, call 06-6982-3114 or visit www.vatican.va (select "Prefecture of the Papal Household"). On Sunday, the pope often gives a blessing at noon (except in July and August) from his apartment overlooking St. Peter's Square. No tickets are required—just show up in the square.

On most Wednesdays at 10:00, the pope speaks to large crowds in St. Peter's Square (in winter, it's in a nearby auditorium). You can just show up and observe from the fringes of the square, but to get closer and have a seat, you'll need a (free) advance ticket. Book online at www.stpatricksamericanrome.org, and pick your ticket up at the English-friendly St. Patrick's Church (Via Boncompagni 31, Metro: Termini, tel. 06-8881-8727). Alternatively, get a ticket from the usually crowded Vatican guard station on St. Peter's Square, starting the Monday before the audience.

Other Vatican City Tours: To see the Vatican Gardens, you must book a tour (usually a few days in advance) at www.museivaticani.va (€32). To see St. Peter's actual tomb beneath the church, you must book a "Necropolis" tour months in advance (€13; see instructions at www.vatican.va—search for "Excavations Office").

Length of This Tour: Allow one hour, plus another hour if you climb the dome (or a half-hour to the roof).

Checkroom: Free and mandatory for bags larger than a daypack.

Starring: Michelangelo, Bernini, St. Peter, a heavenly host...and, occasionally, the pope.

THE TOUR BEGINS

▶ *Find a shady spot where you like the view under the columns around St. Peter's oval-shaped "square." If the pigeons left a clean spot, sit on it.*

Background

Nearly 2,000 years ago, this area was the site of Nero's Circus—a huge cigar-shaped Roman chariot racecourse located just to the left of where St. Peter's is today. The Romans had no marching bands, so for halftime entertainment they killed Christians. Some were crucified, some fed to lions, while others were covered in tar, tied to posts, and burned—human torches to light up the evening races.

One of those crucified here, in about A.D. 65, was Peter, Jesus' right-hand man, who had come to Rome to spread the message of love. His remains were buried in a nearby cemetery located where the main altar in St. Peter's is today. For 250 years, these relics were quietly and secretly revered.

When Christianity was finally legalized in 313, the Christian emperor Constantine built a church on the site of Peter's martyrdom. "Old St. Peter's" lasted 1,200 years (A.D. 326-1500).

By the time of the Renaissance, Old St. Peter's was falling apart and was considered unfit to be the center of the Western Church. The new, larger church we see today was begun in 1506 by the architect Bramante. He was succeeded by a number of different architects, including Michelangelo, who designed the magnificent dome. The church was finally finished in 1626.

▶ *More on the church later—for now, let's talk about the square.*

St. Peter's Square

St. Peter's Square, with its ring of columns, symbolizes the arms of the church welcoming everyone—believers and non-believers—with its motherly embrace. It was designed a century after Michelangelo by the Baroque architect Gian Lorenzo Bernini, who did much of the work that we'll see inside.

Numbers first: 284 columns, 56 feet high, in stern Doric style. Topping them are Bernini's 140 favorite saints, each 10 feet tall. The "square" itself is actually elliptical, 660 by 500 feet. It's a little higher around the edges so that even when full of crowds, those on the periphery can see above the throngs.

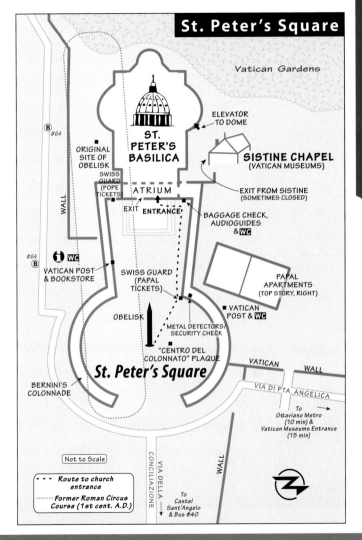

St. Peter's Square

Vatican Gardens

ELEVATOR TO DOME

ST. PETER'S BASILICA

SISTINE CHAPEL (VATICAN MUSEUMS)

(B) #64

ORIGINAL SITE OF OBELISK

SWISS GUARD (POPE TICKETS)

ATRIUM

EXIT FROM SISTINE (SOMETIMES CLOSED)

EXIT **ENTRANCE**

BAGGAGE CHECK, AUDIOGUIDES & WC

WALL

#64 (B) **ℹ WC**

VATICAN POST & BOOKSTORE

SWISS GUARD (PAPAL TICKETS)

PAPAL APARTMENTS (TOP STORY, RIGHT)

VATICAN POST & WC

OBELISK

METAL DETECTORS/ SECURITY CHECK

"CENTRO DEL COLONNATO" PLAQUE

VATICAN WALL

St. Peter's Square

VIA DI PTA. ANGELICA

BERNINI'S COLONNADE

To Ottaviano Metro (10 min) & Vatican Museums Entrance (15 min)

Not to Scale

- - - Route to church entrance
········· Former Roman Circus Course (1st cent. A.D.)

VIA DELLA CONCILIAZIONE

To Castel Sant'Angelo & Bus #40

The **obelisk** in the center is 90 feet of solid granite weighing more than 300 tons. Think of how much history this monument has seen. Originally erected in Egypt more than 2,000 years ago, it witnessed the fall of the pharaohs to the Greeks and then to the Romans. Then the emperor Caligula moved it to imperial Rome. In Nero's day, it stood in the center of his chariot race course (about 100 yards east of its current location), where Christians were slaughtered. As Rome fell and Christians triumphed, the obelisk was moved to this spot (in 1586) and topped with a cross. Today, it watches over the church, a reminder that each civilization builds on the previous ones.

▶ *Venture out across the burning desert to the obelisk, which provides a narrow sliver of shade.*

As you face the church, the gray building to the right at two o'clock, rising up behind Bernini's colonnade is, at least officially, the **pope's abode.** The last window on the right of the top floor is the bedroom. To the left of that window is the study window, where popes have appeared to to greet the masses. Pope Francis, however, has shunned the grand papal

St. Peter's—built on the grave of Jesus' right-hand man, and now the center of Catholicism

apartments and lives instead in a modest Vatican guesthouse. On more formal occasions (which you may have seen on TV), the pope appears from the church itself, on the small balcony above the central door.

The Sistine Chapel is just to the right of the facade—the small gray-brown building with the triangular roof, topped by an antenna. The tiny chimney (the pimple along the roofline midway up the left side) is where the famous smoke signals announce the election of each new pope. If the smoke is black, a two-thirds majority hasn't been reached. White smoke means a new pope has been selected.

Walk to the right, five pavement plaques from the obelisk, to one marked *Centro del Colonnato.* From here, all of Bernini's columns on the right side line up.

▶ *Now make your way up toward the security checkpoint. After clearing security, continue up, passing the huge statues of St. Paul (with his two-edged sword) and St. Peter (with his bushy hair and keys).*

Notice that there are two entrances into Vatican City: one to the left of the facade, and one to the right in the crook of Bernini's "arm." Guarding this small but powerful country's border crossing are the mercenary guards from Switzerland. You have to wonder if they really know how to use those pikes. Their colorful uniforms are said to have been designed by Michelangelo, though he was not known for his sense of humor.

▶ *Enter the narthex (entrance hall) of the church.*

THE BASILICA

The Narthex

The narthex (portico) is itself bigger than most churches. The huge white columns on the portico date from Old St. Peter's (fourth century). Five famous bronze doors lead into the church.

The central door, made from the melted-down bronze of the original door of Old St. Peter's, is only opened on special occasions.

The far-right entrance is the ❶ **Holy Door,** opened only during Holy Years (and special "Jubilee" years designated by the pope). On Christmas Eve every 25 years, the pope knocks three times with a silver hammer and the door opens, welcoming pilgrims to pass through. After Pope John Paul II opened the door on Christmas Eve, 1999, he bricked it up again with a ceremonial trowel a year later to wait another 24 years.

The papal apartments overlook the Square.

The Vatican's Swiss Guard

Then—surprise!—Pope Francis decided to open it from late 2015 to late 2016 for a special Jubilee Year. On the door, note crucified Jesus' shiny knees, polished by pious pilgrims who touch them for a blessing.

▶ *Now for one of Europe's great "wow" experiences. Enter the church. Gape for a while. But don't gape at Michelangelo's famous* Pietà *(on the right). That's this tour's finale. Start by taking in the vast interior.*

The Nave

This church is appropriately huge. Size before beauty: The golden window at the far end is two football fields away. The bronze canopy over the main altar is the size of a seven-story building. The babies at the base of the pillars along the main hall (the nave) are adult-size. The lettering in the gold band along the top of the pillars is seven feet high. Really. The church covers six acres, and can accommodate 60,000 standing worshippers (or 1,200 tour groups).

The church is huge, but everything is designed to make it seem smaller and more intimate than it really is. For example, the statue of St. Teresa near the bottom of the first pillar on the right is 15 feet tall. The statue above her near the top looks the same size, but is actually six feet taller, giving the impression that it's not so far away.

The nave gives a sense of the splendor of ancient Rome that was carried on by the Catholic Church. The floor plan—with a large central aisle (nave) flanked by two side aisles—is based on the ancient Roman basilica, or law-court building.

On the floor near the central doorway, find a round slab of porphyry stone in the maroon color of ancient Roman officials. This is the spot where, on Christmas night in A.D. 800, the king of the Franks ❷ **Charlemagne**

St. Peter's Basilica

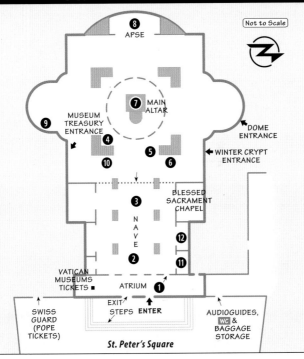

Not to Scale

APSE

MUSEUM TREASURY ENTRANCE

MAIN ALTAR

DOME ENTRANCE

WINTER CRYPT ENTRANCE

BLESSED SACRAMENT CHAPEL

N A V E

VATICAN MUSEUMS TICKETS

ATRIUM

SWISS GUARD (POPE TICKETS)

EXIT STEPS ENTER

AUDIOGUIDES, WC & BAGGAGE STORAGE

St. Peter's Square

❶ Holy Door

❷ Charlemagne's Coronation Site

❸ Extent of Original "Greek Cross" Plan

❹ St. Andrew Statue; View of Dome; Crypt Entrance

❺ St. Peter Statue (with Kissable Toe)

❻ Pope John XXIII

❼ Main Altar (under Bernini's Canopy & over Peter's Tomb)

❽ BERNINI–Dove Window & Throne of St. Peter

❾ St. Peter's Crucifixion Site

❿ RAPHAEL–Mosaic copy of The Transfiguration

⓫ MICHELANGELO–Pietà

⓬ Tomb of St. Pope John Paul II

was crowned Holy Roman Emperor. Even in the Dark Ages—when Rome was virtually abandoned and visitors reported that the city had more thieves and wolves than decent people—St. Peter's was the symbolic center of Europe.

St. Peter's was very expensive to build. The popes financed it by selling "indulgences," allowing the rich to buy forgiveness for their sins. This kind of corruption inspired an obscure German monk named Martin Luther to rebel and start the Protestant Reformation.

The ornate, Baroque-style interior decoration—a riot of marble, gold, stucco, mosaics, columns of stone, and pillars of light—was part of the Church's "Counter-" Reformation. Baroque served as cheery propaganda, impressing followers with the authority of the Church, and giving them a glimpse of the heaven that awaited the faithful.

▶ *Now, walk straight up the center of the nave toward the altar.*

The nave of St. Peter's—two football fields long—can accommodate 60,000 worshippers.

From Pope to Pope

When a pope dies—or retires—the tiny, peaceful Vatican stirs from its timeless slumber and becomes headline news. Millions of people converge on Vatican City, and hundreds of millions around the world watch anxiously on TV.

A deceased pope's body is displayed in state in front of the main altar in St. Peter's Basilica. Thousands of pilgrims line up down Via della Conciliazione, waiting for one last look at their pope. On the day of the funeral, hundreds of thousands of mourners, dignitaries, and security personnel gather in St. Peter's Square. The pope's coffin is carried out to the square, where a eulogy is given.

Most popes are laid to rest in the crypt below St. Peter's Basilica, near the tomb of St. Peter and among shrines to many other popes. Especially popular popes—such as John Paul II or John XXIII—may eventually find a place upstairs, inside St. Peter's itself.

While the previous pope is being laid to rest, cardinals representing Catholics around the globe descend on Rome to elect a new pope. Once they've assembled, the 100-plus cardinals, dressed in crimson, are stripped of their mobile phones, given a vow of secrecy, and locked inside the Sistine Chapel. This begins the "conclave" (from Latin *cum clave*, with key). As they cast votes with paper ballots, the used ballots are burned in a stove temporarily set up inside the Sistine Chapel. The smoke rises up and out the tiny chimney, visible from St. Peter's Square. Black smoke means they haven't yet agreed on a new pope. Finally, the anxious crowd in St. Peter's Square looks up to see a puff of white smoke emerging from the Sistine Chapel. The bells in St. Peter's clock towers ring out gloriously (a new tradition) confirming that, indeed, a pope has been elected. The crowd erupts in cheers, and Romans watching on their TVs hail taxis to hurry to the square.

On the balcony of St. Peter's facade, the newly elected pope steps up and raises his hands, as thousands chant *"Viva il Papa."* A cardinal introduces him to the crowd, announcing his newly chosen name. "Brothers and sisters," the cardinal says in several languages, *"Habemus Papam."* "We have a pope."

❸ "Michelangelo's Church"—The Greek Cross

The plaques on the floor show where other, smaller churches of the world would end if they were placed inside St. Peter's: St. Paul's Cathedral in London (Londinense), Florence's Duomo, and so on.

You'll also walk over circular golden grates. Stop at the second one (at the third pillar from the entrance). Look back at the entrance and realize that if Michelangelo had had his way, this whole long section of the church wouldn't exist. The nave was extended after his death.

Michelangelo was 71 years old when the pope persuaded him to take over the church project and cap it with a dome. He put the dome over Donato Bramante's original "Greek Cross" floor plan, with four equal arms, symbolic of the orderliness of the created world and the perfection of man. But after Michelangelo's death, the Church—struggling against Protestants and its own corruption—opted for a Latin cross plan, designed to impress the world with its grandeur.

Michelangelo's dome—448 feet tall—hovers directly above the altar and St. Peter's tomb.

▶ *Continue toward the altar, entering "Michelangelo's Church." Park yourself in front of the* ❹ *statue of St. Andrew to the left of the altar.*

The Dome

The dome soars higher than a football field on end, 448 feet from the floor of the cathedral to the top of the lantern. It glows with light from its windows, the blue and gold mosaics creating a cool, solemn atmosphere. In this majestic vision of heaven (not painted by Michelangelo), we see (above the windows) Jesus, Mary, and a ring of saints, more rings of angels above them, and, way up in the ozone, God the Father (a blur of blue and red without binoculars). When Michelangelo died (1564), he'd completed only the drum of the dome—the base up to the windows flanked by half-columns—but the next architects were guided by his designs.

Listen to the hum of visitors echoing through St. Peter's and reflect on our place in the cosmos: half animal, half angel, stretched between heaven and earth, born to live only a short while, a bubble of foam on a great cresting wave of humanity.

▶ *But I digress.*

Peter

The base of the dome is ringed with a gold banner telling us in massive blue letters why this church is so important. According to Catholics, Peter was selected by Jesus to head the church. The banner (in Latin) quotes from the Bible where Jesus says to him, "You are Peter *(Tu es Petrus)* and upon this rock I will build my church, and to you I will give the keys of the kingdom of heaven" (Matthew 16:18).

Peter became the first bishop of Rome. His prestige and that of the

St. Andrew gazes up at the dome: "Wow!"

"Tu es Petrus"—You are Peter...

Peter, the "Fisher of Men"

According to the Bible, Peter was a fisherman who was chosen by Christ to catch sinners instead. This "fisher of men" had human weaknesses that have endeared him to Christians. He was the disciple who tried to walk on water—but failed. In another incident, he impetuously cut off a man's ear when soldiers came to arrest Jesus. And he even denied knowing Christ, to save his own skin. But Jesus chose him anyway, and gave him his nickname—Rock (in Latin: *Petrus*).

Venerable bronze statue of Peter

Legends say that Peter came to the wicked city of Rome after Jesus' death to spread the gospel of love. He may have been imprisoned for his faith, and other stories claim he had a vision of Christ along the Appian Way (✪ see page 153). Eventually, Peter's preaching offended Emperor Nero. Christ's fisherman was arrested, crucified upside-down, and buried here, where St. Peter's now stands.

city itself made this bishopric more illustrious than all others, and Peter's authority has supposedly passed in an unbroken chain to each succeeding bishop of Rome—that is, the 260-odd popes that followed.

Under the dome, under the bronze canopy, under the altar, some 23 feet under the marble floor, rest the bones of St. Peter, the "rock" upon which this particular church was built. You can't see the tomb, but go to the railing and look down into the small, **lighted niche** below the altar. This niche holds a box containing bishops' shawls—a symbol of how Peter's authority spread to the other churches. Peter's tomb (not visible) is just below this box.

Are they really the bones of Jesus' apostle? According to a papal pronouncement: definitely maybe. The traditional site of his tomb was sealed up when Old St. Peter's was built on it in A.D. 326. In 1940, the tomb was opened for archaeological study. Bones were found, dated from the first century, of a robust man who died in old age. His body was wrapped in expensive cloth. Various inscriptions and graffiti in the tomb indicate that second- and third-century visitors thought this was Peter's tomb. Does that mean it's really Peter? Who am I to disagree with the pope? Definitely maybe.

If you line up the cross on the altar with the dove in the window, you'll notice that the niche below the cross is just off-center compared with the rest of the church. Why? Because Michelangelo built the church around the traditional location of the tomb, not the actual location—about two feet away—discovered by modern archaeology.

Back in the nave sits a ❺ **bronze statue of Peter** under a canopy that dates from Old St. Peter's. In one hand he holds the keys, the symbol of the authority given him by Christ, while with the other hand he blesses us. He's wearing a toga. It may be that the original statue was of a Roman senator and that the bushy head and keys were added later to make it Peter. His big right toe has been worn smooth by the lips of pilgrims and foot-fetishists. Stand in line and kiss it, or, to avoid foot-and-mouth disease, touch your hand to your lips, then rub the toe. This is simply an act of reverence with no legend attached, though you can make one up if you like.

▸ *Circle to the right around the statue of Peter to find another popular stop among pilgrims: the lighted glass niche with the red-robed body of* ❻ **Pope John XXIII** *(reigned 1958-1963). Now known as Saint John, it was he who initiated the landmark Vatican II Council (1962-1965) that instituted major reforms, bringing the Church into the modern age.*

❼ The Main Altar

The main altar beneath the dome and canopy (the white marble slab with cross and candlesticks) is used only when the pope himself says Mass. He sometimes conducts the Sunday morning service when he's in town, a sight worth seeing. I must admit, though, it's a little strange being frisked at the door for weapons at the holiest place in Christendom.

The tiny altar would be lost in this enormous church if it weren't for Gian Lorenzo Bernini's seven-story bronze canopy (God's "four-poster bed"), which "extends" the altar upward and reduces the perceived distance between floor and ceiling. The corkscrew columns echo the marble ones that surrounded the altar/tomb in Old St. Peter's. Some of the bronze used here was taken and melted down from the ancient Pantheon.

Bernini's bronze canopy rises above the main altar, creating a proscenium for the Mass.

Bernini (1598-1680), the Michelangelo of the Baroque era, is the man most responsible for the interior decoration of the church. As an architect, sculptor, and painter, Bernini was uniquely qualified to turn St. Peter's into a multimedia extravaganza. Nowhere is there such a conglomeration of works by the flamboyant genius who remade the church—and the city—in the Baroque style.

The altar area was his masterpiece, a "theater" for holy spectacles. Besides the bronze canopy, Bernini did the statue of lance-bearing St. Longinus ("The hills are alive..."), the balconies above the four statues, and much of the marble floor decoration. Bernini gave an impressive unity to a diverse variety of pillars, windows, statues, aisles, and chapels.

▶ *Approach the apse, the front area with the golden dove window.*

The Apse

Bernini's ⑧ **dove window** shines above the smaller front altar used for everyday services. The Holy Spirit, in the form of a six-foot-high dove, pours sunlight onto the faithful through the alabaster windows, turning into artificial rays of gold and reflecting off swirling gold clouds, angels, and winged babies. During a service, real sunlight passes through real clouds of incense, mingling with Bernini's sculpture. This is the epitome of Baroque—an ornate, mixed-media work designed to overwhelm the viewer.

Beneath the dove is the centerpiece of this structure, the so-called **Throne of St. Peter,** an oak chair built in medieval times for a king. Subsequently, it was encrusted with tradition and encased in bronze by Bernini as a symbol of papal authority. Statues of four early Church Fathers support the chair, a symbol of how bishops should support the pope in troubled times—times like the Counter-Reformation.

The dove window designed by Bernini

Sunbeams often light the afternoon service.

Pope Francis I

In 2013, Jorge Bergoglio of Argentina became Francis I, the church's 266th pope.
Francis (b. 1936) grew up in Buenos Aires
in a family of working-class Italian immi-
grants. He spent his twenties in various
jobs (chemist, high-school teacher) before
entering the priesthood and eventually
becoming Archbishop of Buenos Aires.

Pope Francis represents three "firsts"
that signal a new direction for the Church. As the first pope from the
Americas, Francis personifies the 80 percent of Catholics who now
live outside Europe. As the first Jesuit pope—from the religious order
known for education—he stands for spreading the faith through teach-
ing, not aggression. And as the first Francis—named after St. Francis of
Assisi—he calls to mind that medieval friar's efforts to return a corrupt
church to simple Christian values of poverty and humility. Having
taken the helm after the previous pope had retired (not died), Francis
shares the world stage with "pope emeritus" Benedict.

Like his namesake Francis, the pope lives simply. He resides in a
Vatican guest house rather than the official Papal Apartments overlooking St. Peter's Square. He reportedly eats leftovers.

When people talk about Francis, the word that comes up time and
again is… "dialogue." He's known for listening to every point of view,
whether it's mediating between dictators and union leaders, sitting
down with the Orthodox Patriarch, celebrating Rosh Hashanah with
Jews, or visiting a mosque. He speaks a number of languages, including fluent Italian—the language of his parents and of the Vatican.

No one expects Francis to institute major changes in church
doctrine. But he's completely changed the church's image. He's attacked rich capitalists (the Church's main donors), and cast his lot with
society's poor and outcast. He's embraced gays and praised atheists.
Francis wants to de-emphasize the divisive "culture war" issues in
order to reach out to a global audience. As Francis himself has pointed
out, the original Latin word for pope—"pontifex"—literally means
"bridge-builder."

Remember that St. Peter's is a church, not a museum. In the apse, Mass is said for pilgrims, tourists, and Roman citizens alike. Wooden confessional booths are available for Catholics to tell their sins to a listening ear and receive forgiveness and peace of mind. The faithful renew their faith, and the faithless gain inspiration. Look at the light streaming through the windows, turn and gaze up into the dome, and quietly contemplate your deity (or lack thereof).

▶ *To the left of the main altar is the south transept. (The transept is sometimes closed to all but worshippers. Anyone who indicates to the guard that they wish to pray can enter.) At the far end, left side, find the dark "painting" of St. Peter crucified upside-down.*

❾ Peter's Crucifixion Site

Because smoke and humidity would damage real paintings, this and all the other "paintings" in the church are actually mosaic copies made from thousands of colored chips the size of your little fingernail.

This work marks the exact spot (according to tradition) where Peter was killed 1,900 years ago. Peter had come to the world's greatest city to preach Jesus' message of love to the pagan, often hostile Romans. During the reign of Nero, he was arrested and brought to Nero's Circus so all Rome could witness his execution. When the authorities told Peter he was to be crucified just like his Lord, Peter said "I'm not worthy" and insisted they nail him on the cross upside-down.

The Romans were actually quite tolerant of other religions, but monotheistic Christians refused to worship the Roman emperor even when burned alive, thrown to the lions, or crucified. Their bravery, optimism in suffering, and message of love struck a chord with slaves and the lower classes. The religion started by a poor carpenter grew, despite persecution by fanatical emperors. In three short centuries, Christianity went from a small Jewish sect in Jerusalem to the official religion of the world's greatest empire.

Around the corner on the right, pause at the mosaic copy of Raphael's epic painting of ❿ **The Transfiguration.**

▶ *Back near the entrance to the church, in the far corner, behind bulletproof glass, is the...*

⓫ *Pietà*

Michelangelo was 24 years old when he completed this *Pietà* (pee-ay-TAH) of Mary mourning the dead body of Christ taken from the cross. It was

Michelangelo's first major commission (by the French ambassador to the Vatican), done for Holy Year 1500.

Pietà means "pity." Michelangelo, with his total mastery of the real world, captures the sadness of the moment. Mary cradles her crucified son in her lap. Christ's lifeless right arm drooping down lets us know how heavy this corpse is. His smooth skin is accented by the rough folds of Mary's robe. Mary tilts her head down, looking at her dead son with sad tenderness. Her left hand turns upward, asking, "How could they do this to you?"

Michelangelo didn't think of sculpting as creating a figure, but as simply freeing the God-made figure from the prison of marble around it. He'd attack a project like this with an inspired passion, chipping away to find what God had placed inside.

The bunched-up shoulder and rigor-mortis legs show that Michelangelo learned well from his studies of cadavers. But realistic as this work

The *Pieta,* by 24-year-old Michelangelo, was one of the rare statues he polished to perfection.

is, its true power lies in the subtle "unreal" features. Life-size Christ looks childlike compared with larger-than-life Mary. Unnoticed at first, this accentuates the subconscious impression of Mary enfolding Jesus in her maternal love. Mary—the mother of a 33-year-old man—looks like a teenager, emphasizing how Mary was the eternally youthful "handmaiden" of the Lord, always serving God's will, even if it meant giving up her son.

The statue is a solid pyramid of maternal tenderness. Yet within this, Christ's body tilts diagonally down to the right, and Mary's hem flows with it. Subconsciously, we feel the weight of this dead God sliding from her lap to the ground.

At 11:30 on May 23, 1972, a madman with a hammer entered St. Peter's and began hacking away at the *Pietà*. The damage was repaired, but that's why there's now a shield of bulletproof glass.

This is Michelangelo's only signed work. The story goes that he overheard some pilgrims praising his finished *Pietà*, but attributing it to a second-rate sculptor from a lesser city. He was so enraged that he grabbed his chisel and chipped "Michelangelo Buonarroti of Florence did this" in the ribbon running down Mary's chest.

On your right (covered in gray concrete with a gold cross) is the inside of the Holy Door. If there's a prayer inside you, ask that—when this door is next opened in 2025—St. Peter's will no longer need security checks or bulletproof glass, and pilgrims will enter in peace.

The Rest of the Church

⑫ **Tomb of Pope John Paul II (Chapel of San Sebastian):** The tomb of Pope John Paul II (1920-2005) was moved to the chapel of San Sebastian in 2011, after he was beatified by Pope Benedict XVI. Now Saint John Paul, he lies beneath a painting of his favorite saint, the steadfast St. Sebastian.

The Crypt (a.k.a. Grotte, or Tombe): The entrance to the church's "basement" is usually beside the statue of St. Andrew, to the left of the main altar. You descend to the floor level of Old St. Peter's. You see tombs of popes, including Paul VI (1963-1978), who suffered through the church's modernization. The finale is the unimpressive "sepulcher of Peter," a ceremonial chapel and niche honoring Peter's tomb, which is located behind the niche (and which you can't see). The walk through the Crypt is free and quick (15 minutes), but you won't see St. Peter's original grave unless you take a *Scavi* (excavations) tour. You'll end up, usually, near the checkroom.

Vatican City

This tiny, independent country of little more than 100 acres, contained entirely within Rome, has its own postal system, armed guards, helipad, mini-train station, radio station (KPOP), and euro coin (featuring the pope). Politically powerful, the Vatican is the religious capital of 1.2 billion Roman Catholics. If you're not a Catholic, become one for your visit.

The pope is both the religious and secular leader of Vatican City. The city is the last remnant of the once-powerful Papal States of central Italy, ruled by popes since the fall of Rome. When modern Italy was created in 1870, the Papal States became part of the nation of Italy, and the Italian government tried to gain control of Vatican City. It wasn't until 1929's Lateran Pact that Italy and the pope officially recognized each other's government, assuring Vatican City's independence.

Treasury Museum (Museo-Tesoro): The museum, located on the left side of the nave near the altar, contains the room-size tomb of Sixtus IV by Antonio Pollaiuolo, a big pair of Roman pincers used to torture Christians, an original corkscrew column from Old St. Peter's, and assorted jewels, papal robes, and golden reliquaries—a marked contrast to the poverty of early Christians.

Blessed Sacrament Chapel: Worshippers are welcome to step through the metalwork gates into this oasis of peace located on the right-hand side of the church, about midway to the altar.

Up to the Dome (Cupola)

A good way to finish a visit to St. Peter's is to go up into the dome for the best view of Rome anywhere (open daily April-Sept 8:00-17:00, Oct-March 8:00-16:00). The entrance to the dome is along the right side of the church, but the line begins to form on the church's front steps, near the right door of the main facade (follow signs to *cupola*).

First, you take the elevator or climb 231 stairs to the church roof, just above the facade. From the roof, you have a commanding view of St. Peter's Square, the statues on the colonnade, Rome across the Tiber in front of you, and the dome itself—almost terrifying in its nearness—looming behind you. This view from the roof may only be accessible after you've descended from the dome—the route changes.

From here, you can also go inside, to the gallery ringing the interior of the dome, where you can look down inside the church. Study the mosaics up close—and those huge letters! Survey the top of Bernini's seven-story-tall canopy, and wonder how (or if) they ever dust it. It's worth the elevator ride for this view alone.

From roof level, if you're energetic, continue all the way up to the top of the dome. The staircase actually winds between the outer shell and the inner one. It's a sweaty, crowded, claustrophobic 15-minute, 323-step climb, but worth it.

The view from the summit is great, the fresh air even better. Admire the arms of Bernini's colonnade encircling St. Peter's Square. Find the big, white Victor Emmanuel Monument, with the two statues on top. Nearby is the Pantheon, with its large, light, shallow dome. The large rectangular building to the left of the obelisk is the Vatican Museums, stuffed with art. Survey the Vatican grounds, with its mini-train system and lush gardens. Look down into the square on the tiny pilgrims buzzing like electrons around the nucleus of Catholicism.

It's a sweaty 323-step climb to the top of the dome, but the view is heavenly.

Borghese Gallery Tour

Galleria e Museo Borghese

More than just a great museum, the Borghese Gallery is a beautiful villa set in the greenery of surrounding gardens. You get to see art commissioned by the luxury-loving Borghese family displayed in the very rooms for which it was created.

There's a superb collection of works by Bernini, including his intricately carved *Apollo and Daphne,* a statue that's more air than stone. Among the many Caravaggio paintings is the artist's portrait of himself—as a severed head. Frescoes, marble, stucco, and interior design enhance the masterpieces.

This is a place where—regardless of whether you learn a darn thing— you can sit back and enjoy the sheer beauty of the palace and its art.

ORIENTATION

Cost: €11 (see "Reservations" below); free and very crowded first Sun of the month.

Hours: Tue-Sun 9:00-19:00, closed Mon.

Reservations: Reservations are mandatory and simple to get. Choose your day and an entry time at 9:00, 11:00, 13:00, 15:00, or 17:00. Booking online is easiest (www.tosc.it, €4 extra booking fee). You can also reserve by phone (tel. 06-32810, press 2 for English; office hours: Mon-Fri 9:00-18:00, Sat 9:00-13:00, closed Sat in Aug and Sun year-round). To pick up your ticket, present your claim number at the Borghese entrance 30 minutes before your appointed entry time (or risk forfeiting your reservation).

During peak season (May-Sept), reserve a minimum of several days in advance for a weekday visit, and at least a week ahead for weekends. In winter, you may be able to get tickets on shorter notice.

Getting There: The museum is set idyllically but inconveniently in the vast Villa Borghese Gardens. A taxi drops you 100 yards from the museum (tell the cabbie "gal-leh-REE-ah bor-GAY-zay"). Bus #910 goes from Termini train station to the Via Pinciana stop, 100 yards from the museum. By Metro, use the Barberini stop, walk up Via Veneto, enter the park, and turn right, following signs (a 20-minute walk). The Spagna Metro stop is equally close, but the route to the museum is circuitous.

Information: Piazzale del Museo Borghese 5, tel. 06-32810 (ticket service) or 06-841-3979 (museum), www.galleriaborghese.it.

Tours: €6.50 guided English tours are offered at 9:00 and 11:00. Sign up as soon as you arrive. The €5 audioguide is excellent.

Museum Strategy: Visits are strictly limited to two hours. Budget most of your time for the more interesting ground floor, but set aside 30 minutes for the paintings of the Pinacoteca upstairs. Avoid the crowds by seeing the Pinacoteca first.

Bag Check: It's free, mandatory, and strictly enforced. Even small purses must be checked. The checkroom does not take coats.

Photography: Allowed without flash.

Cuisine Art: A café is on-site. The sandwich chain VyTA has a location at Casa del Cinema within the park, a pleasant 10-minute walk directly

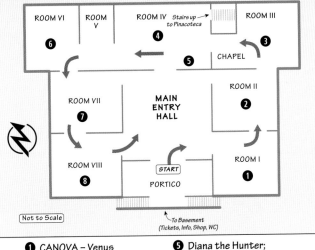

Borghese Gallery—Ground Floor

ROOM VI

ROOM V

ROOM IV   Stairs up to Pinacoteca

ROOM III

CHAPEL

ROOM VII

MAIN ENTRY HALL

ROOM II

ROOM VIII

START
PORTICO

ROOM I

Not to Scale

To Basement
(Tickets, Info, Shop, WC)

❶ CANOVA – Venus

❷ BERNINI – David

❸ BERNINI – Apollo and Daphne

❹ BERNINI – The Rape of Proserpine

❺ Diana the Hunter; other marbles

❻ BERNINI – Aeneas

❼ "Theater of the Universe"

❽ CARAVAGGIO – Various

downhill from the museum, near the bike-rental stand. Or, buy a picnic beforehand, check it with your bag, and feast afterward in the picnic-friendly park.

Starring: Sculptures by Bernini; Canova's Venus; paintings by Caravaggio, Raphael, and Titian; and the elegant villa itself.

THE TOUR BEGINS

As you visit this palace-in-a-garden, consider its purpose. Cardinal Scipione Borghese (1576-1633) landscaped the sprawling Villa Borghese Gardens, built the villa, hired the best artists of his day to decorate it, and filled it with his collection of ancient works—all so he could wine and dine Rome's VIPs and show off his fine art. In pursuing the optimistic spirit of the Renaissance, they invented Baroque.

▶ *Enter on the ground floor, passing into the large, impressive...*

Main Entry Hall

Guests would enter and be wowed by a multimedia extravaganza of art. Baroque frescoes on the ceiling, Greek statues along the walls, and ancient Roman mosaics on the floor capture the essence of the collection—a gathering of beautiful objects from every age and culture.

Five mosaics from a private Roman villa (second- and third-century A.D.) adorn the floor with colorful, festive scenes of slaughter. Gladiators—as famous in their day as the sports heroes of our age—fight animals and each other with swords, whips, and tridents. The Greek letter "Θ" marks the dead. Notice some of the gladiators' pro-wrestler nicknames: "Cupid(-o)," "Serpent(-ius)," "Licentious(-us)." On the far left a scene shows how "Alumnus" killed "Mazicinus" and left him lying upside down in a pool of blood.

High up on the wall is a thrilling first-century Greek sculpture of a horse falling. The Renaissance-era rider was added by Pietro Bernini, father of the famous Gian Lorenzo Bernini.

▶ *Turn right and enter Room I.*

❶ Antonio Canova—*Pauline Borghese as Venus* (*Paolina Borghese come Venere*, 1808)

Napoleon's sister went the full monty for the sculptor Canova, scandalizing Europe. ("How could you have done such a thing?!" she was asked. She replied, "The room wasn't cold.") With the famous nose of her conqueror brother, she strikes the pose of Venus as conqueror of men's hearts. Her relaxed afterglow and slight smirk say she's already had her man. The light dent she puts in the mattress makes this goddess human.

Notice the contrasting textures that Canova (1757-1822) gets out of the pure white marble: the rumpled sheet versus her smooth skin, the

Canova's cool *Venus* lounges across a rumpled mattress of marble.

satiny-smooth pillows and mattress versus the creases in them, her porcelain skin versus the hint of a love handle. Canova polished and waxed the marble until it looked as soft and pliable as cloth.

The mythological pose, the Roman couch, the ancient hairdo, and the calm harmony make Pauline the epitome of the Neoclassical style.

▶ *Continue into Room II.*

❷ Gian Lorenzo Bernini—*David* (1624)

Duck! David twists around to put a big rock in his sling. He purses his lips, knits his brow, and winds his body like a spring as his eyes lock onto the target—Goliath, who's somewhere behind us, putting us right in the line of fire.

In this self-portrait, 25-year-old Bernini (1598-1680) is ready to take on the world. He's charged with the same fighting energy that fueled the missionaries and conquistadors of the Counter-Reformation.

Compared with Michelangelo's *David,* this is unvarnished realism—an unbalanced pose, bulging veins, unflattering face, and armpit hair. Michelangelo's *David* thinks, whereas Bernini's acts—with lips pursed,

Bernini portrays himself as *David,* the giant-slayer ready to take on the world.

eyes concentrating, and sling stretched. Bernini slays the pretty boy Davids of the Renaissance and prepares to invent Baroque.

▶ *Continue into Room III.*

❸ Bernini—*Apollo and Daphne (Apollo e Dafne,* 1625)

Apollo—made stupid by Cupid's arrow of love—chases after Daphne, who has been turned off by the "arrow of disgust." Just as he's about to catch her, she calls to her father to save her. Magically, her fingers begin to sprout leaves, her toes become roots, her skin turns to bark, and she transforms into a tree. Frustrated Apollo will end up with a handful of leaves.

Stand behind the statue to experience it as Bernini originally intended. It's only when you circle around to the front that he reveals the story's surprise ending.

Walk slowly around the statue. Apollo's back leg defies gravity. Bernini has chipped away more than half of the block of marble, leaving airy, open spaces. The statue spent two years in restoration (described to me as similar to dental work). The marble leaves at the top ring like crystal when struck. Notice the same scene, colorized, painted on the ceiling above.

Bernini carves out some of the chief features of Baroque art. He makes a supernatural event seem realistic. He freezes it at the most dramatic, emotional moment. The figures move and twist in unusual poses. He turns the wind machine on, sending Apollo's cape billowing behind him. It's a sculpture group of two, forming a scene, rather than a stand-alone portrait. And the subject is classical. Even in strict Counter-Reformation times, there was always a place for groping, if the subject matter had a moral—this one taught you not to pursue fleeting earthly pleasures. And, besides, Bernini tends to show a lot of skin, but no genitals.

▶ *Pass through the cardinal's private chapel and into Room IV.*

❹ Bernini—*The Rape of Proserpina (Il Ratto di Proserpina,* 1622)

Pluto, King of the Underworld, strides into his realm and shows off his catch—the beautiful daughter of the earth goddess. His three-headed guard dog Cerberus (who guards the gates of hell), barks triumphantly. Pluto is squat, thick, and uncouth, with knotted muscles and untrimmed beard. He's trying not to hurt her, but she pushes her divine molester away and twists to call out for help. Tears roll down her cheeks. She wishes she could turn into a tree.

Even at the tender age of 24, Bernini was the master of marble. Look how Pluto's fingers dig into her frantic body as if it were real flesh. Bernini picked out this Carrara marble, knowing that its relative suppleness and ivory hue would lend itself to a fleshy statue. While Renaissance works

Apollo and Daphne—a divine stalker

The Rape of Proserpina—a divine kidnapping

Gian Lorenzo Bernini (1598-1680)

A Renaissance Man in Counter-Reformation times, Bernini almost personally invented the Baroque style, transforming the city of Rome. If you're visiting Rome, you will see Bernini's work, guaranteed.

St. Teresa at S.M. della Vittoria church

Bernini was a child prodigy in his father's sculpting studio, growing up among Europe's rich and powerful. His flamboyant personality endeared him to his cultured employers—the popes in Rome, Louis XIV in France, and Charles I in England. He was extremely prolific, working fast and utilizing an army of assistants.

Despite the fleshiness and sensuality of his works, Bernini was a religious man, seeing his creativity as an extension of God's. In stark contrast to the Protestant world's sobriety, Bernini shamelessly embraced pagan myths and nude goddesses, declaring them all part of the "catholic"—that is, universal—church.

Bernini, a master of multimedia, was a...
- Sculptor (Borghese Gallery and *St. Teresa in Ecstasy*)
- Architect (St. Peter's Square and more)
- Painter (Borghese Gallery)
- Interior decorator (the bronze canopy and more in St. Peter's)
- Civil engineer (fountains in Piazza Navona, Piazza Barberini, Piazza di Spagna, and more).

Even works done by other artists a century later such as the Trevi Fountain can be traced indirectly to Bernini, the man who invented Baroque, the "look" of Rome for the next two centuries.

were designed to be seen from the front, Bernini creates theater-in-the-round—full of action, designed to be experienced as you walk around it.

▶ *Looking around, admire some...*

Other Objects in Room IV

In a niche over Pluto's right shoulder, find a small statue of ❺ **Diana the Hunter.** The goddess has been running through the forest. Now she's spotted her prey, and slows down, preparing to string her (missing) bow with an arrow. Or is she smoking a (missing) cigarette? Scholars debate it. The statue is a second century B.C. Greek original, amazingly intact.

As you peruse the statues, emperor busts, and decoration in this room, appreciate the beauty of the **different types of marble:** Bernini's ivory Carrara, Diana's translucent white, purple porphyry emperors, granite-like columns that support them, wood-grained pilasters on the walls, and the different colors on the floor—green, red, gray, lavender, and yellow, some grainy, some "marbled" like a steak. Some of the world's most beautiful and durable things have been made from the shells of sea creatures layered in sediment, fossilized into limestone, then baked and crystallized by the pressure of the earth—marble.

▶ *Continue on. Pass through one room and pause in Room VI.*

❻ Bernini—*Aeneas, Anchises, and Ascanius* (1618-1619)

Aeneas' home in Troy is in flames, and he escapes with the three most important things: his family (decrepit father on his shoulder, baby boy), his household gods (the statues in dad's hands), and the Eternal Flame (carried by son). They're all in shock, lost in thought, facing an uncertain future. Eventually (according to legend), Aeneas will arrive in Italy, establish the city of Rome, and house the flame in the Temple of Vesta.

Bernini was just 20 when he started this, his first major work for Cardinal Borghese. Bernini's portrayal of human flesh—from baby fat to middle-aged muscle to sagging decrepitude—is astonishing. Still, the flat-footed statue just stands there—it lacks the Baroque energy of his more mature work. More lively are the reliefs up at the ceiling, with their dancing, light-footed soldiers with do-si-do shields.

▶ *Enter Room VII.*

❼ The "Theater of the Universe"

The room's decor sums up the eclectic nature of the villa. There are Greek statues, Roman mosaics, and fake "Egyptian" sphinxes and hieroglyphs. Look out the window past the sculpted gardens at the mesh domes of the aviary, once filled with exotic birds. Cardinal Borghese's vision was to make a place where art, history, music, nature, and science from every place and time would come together..."a theater of the universe."

► *Our final stop on the ground floor is Room VIII.*

❽ Caravaggio

This room holds the greatest collection of Caravaggio paintings anywhere. Caravaggio (1571-1610) brought Christian saints down to earth with gritty realism, using ordinary people as his models.

Trace the course of Caravaggio's brief, dramatic, and sometimes messy life. *Self-Portrait as Bacchus* shows 20-something Caravaggio as he first arrived in Rome, a poor bohemian enjoying the wild life. *Boy with a Fruit Basket* dates from when he eked out a living painting minor figures in other artists' paintings. His specialty? Fruit. Ultra-realistic fruit. In 1600,

The brash young Caravaggio portrays himself as *Bacchus,* the decadent god of wine.

Caravaggio completed his first major commission (for the Church of San Luigi dei Francesi, ✪ see page 134). Overnight, he was famous.

In the next 10 years, Caravaggio pioneered Baroque painting, much as Bernini soon would do with sculpture. Caravaggio's unique style combined two striking elements: uncompromising realism and strong light-dark contrasts. His saints (e.g., *Saint Jerome*) are balding and wrinkled. His models were ordinary people—*St. John the Baptist* is a nude teenager with dirty feet, whose belly fat wrinkles up as he turns. The *Madonna of Palafrenieri* was forbidden to hang in St. Peter's because the boy Jesus was buck naked and the Madonna resembled Rome's best-known prostitute. Caravaggio's figures emerge from a dark background, lit by a harsh, unflattering light, which highlights part of the image, leaving the rest in deep shadows.

Now rich and famous, Caravaggio led a reckless, rock-star existence—trashing hotel rooms and picking fights. In 1606, he killed a man (the details are sketchy), and had to flee Rome. In one of Caravaggio's last paintings, David sticks Goliath's severed head right in our face—and "Goliath" is the artist himself. From exile, Caravaggio appealed to Cardinal Borghese (one of his biggest fans) to get him a pardon. But while returning to Rome, Caravaggio died under mysterious circumstances. Though he only lived to 38, in his short life he'd rocked the world of art.

▶ *Part one of your visit is done. To reach the Pinacoteca (upstairs), head through the main entry hall back to Room IV, find the entry to the staircase in the far right corner, and spiral up. From the top of the stairs, step into the large Room XIV.*

Pinacoteca (Painting Gallery)

Several objects in Room XIV give a clearer picture of the man who built the villa (Cardinal Scipione), and the man who helped decorate it (Bernini).

▶ *Along the long wall, find the following statues and paintings by Bernini. Start with the two identical white busts set on columns.*

❶ Bernini—Busts of Cardinal Borghese (1632)

Say *"grazie"* to the man who built this villa, assembled the collection, and hired Bernini to sculpt masterpieces. The cardinal is caught turning as if greeting someone at a party. There's a twinkle in his eye, and he opens his mouth to make a witty comment.

This man of the cloth was, in fact, a sophisticated (and not terribly

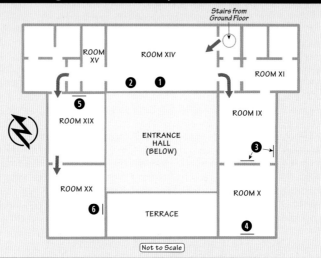

Borghese Gallery—Pinacoteca

❶ BERNINI – Two Busts of
Cardinal Borghese;
Two Self-Portraits;
Bust of Pope Paul V
❷ BERNINI – The Goat
Amalthea with the Child
Jupiter and a Faun
❸ RAPHAEL – Deposition;
Young Woman with Unicorn
❹ CORREGGIO – Danaë
❺ DOMENICHINO – The Hunt
of Diana
❻ TITIAN – Sacred and
Profane Love

religious) hedonist. But as the pope's nephew, he became a cardinal. He used church funds to buy beautiful things, many of which are still on display here in the gallery.

Notice that there are two identical versions of this bust. The first one started cracking along the forehead (visible) just as Bernini was finishing it. No problema—Bernini whipped out a replacement in just three days.

▶ *Between the busts, find these paintings...*

❶ Bernini, Self-Portraits (*Autoritratto Giovanile,* 1623, and *Autoritratto in età Matura,* 1630-1635)

Bernini was a master of many media, including painting. The younger Bernini (age 25) looks out a bit hesitantly, as if he's still finding his way in high-class society. The next self-portrait (age 35) has more confidence and facial hair—the dashing, vibrant man who would rebuild Rome in Baroque style.

▶ *On the table below, find the smaller...*

❶ Bust of Pope Paul V (1618)

Cardinal Scipione's uncle was a more sober man than his nephew. As pope, Paul V ruled over the artistic era of Caravaggio and Bernini. He reopened an ancient aqueduct, helped steer St. Peter's toward completion, and personally met with Galileo to discuss the heliocentrism controversy. (Does the Earth revolve around the Sun—or vice versa?) He was also a patron of the arts with a good eye for talent who hired Bernini's father. When Pope Paul V saw sketches made by little Gian Lorenzo, he announced, "This boy will be the Michelangelo of his age."

▶ *To the right of the Borghese busts, find a small statue of...*

❷ The Goat Amalthea with the Child Jupiter and a Faun (1609/1615)

Bernini was barely entering puberty when he made this. (That's about the age when he mastered how to make a Play-Doh snake.) But already its arrangement takes what would become one of Bernini's trademark forms: the sculptural ensemble. The two kids are milking a goat and drinking the milk. The kids lean one way, the goat the other, with the whole composition contained neatly in a circle of good fun.

▶ *Backtrack to the staircase/elevator and turn right to find Room IX.*

❸ Raphael (Raffaello Sanzio)—Deposition (*Deposizione,* 1507)

Jesus is being taken from the cross. The men support him while the women support Mary (in purple). The woman who commissioned the painting had recently lost her son. We see two different faces of grief: mother Mary faints at the horror, while Mary Magdalene—rushing up to take Christ's hand—still can't quite believe he's gone.

Enjoy the rich colors—solid reds, green, blue, and yellow—that set off Christ's porcelain-skin body. In true Renaissance style, Raphael (1483-1520) orders the scene with geometrical perfection. The curve of Jesus'

Deposition, by Raphael—sacred beauty

Danaë, by Correggio—profane beauty

body is echoed by the swirl of Mary Magdalene's hair, and then by the curve of Calvary Hill, where Christ met his fate.

▶ *See Raphael's lighter side in his playful* Portrait of Young Woman with Unicorn, *then continue into Room X.*

❹ Correggio—*Danae* (c. 1531)

Cupid strips Danae as she spreads her legs, most unladylike, to receive a trickle of gold from the smudgy cloud overhead—this was Zeus' idea of intercourse with a human. The sheets are rumpled, and Danae looks right where the action is with a smile on her face. It's hard to believe that a supposedly religious family would display such an erotic work. But the Borgheses felt that all forms of human expression—including physical passion—glorified God.

▶ *Backtrack through the room with the two cardinal busts, then turn left to find Room XIX. Pause at Domenichino's* ❺ **The Hunt of Diana,** *where half-naked Greek nymphs frolic under the watchful eye of the goddess of the hunt. Then continue frolicking into Room XX to finish with a masterpiece by Titian.*

❻ Titian (Tiziano Vecellio)—*Sacred and Profane Love* (*Amor Sacro e Amor Profano, c. 1515*)

The sacred woman and the profane—which is which?

The naked woman on the right actually embodies sacred love. She has nothing to hide and enjoys open spaces filled with light, life, a church in the distance, and even a couple of lovers in the field.

The material girl who represents profane love is dressed in fine clothes, with her box of treasures, fortified castle, and dark, claustrophobic

Sacred and Profane Love—two women (or are they the same one?) embodying polar opposites

landscape. She is recently married, and she cradles a vase filled with jewels representing the riches of earthly love. Her naked twin on the right holds the burning flame of eternal, heavenly love. Baby Cupid, between them, playfully stirs the waters.

Symbolically, the steeple on the right points up to the love of heaven, while on the left, soldiers prepare to "storm the castle" of the new bride. Miss Heavenly Love looks jealous.

This exquisite painting expresses the spirit of the Renaissance—that earth and heaven are two sides of the same coin. And here in the Borghese Gallery, that love of earthly beauty can be spiritually uplifting—as long as you feel it within two hours.

Sights

Rome itself is its own best sight. Watching Romans go about their everyday business is endlessly fascinating, whether you ever visit a museum or not. Take time to observe how past and present coexist in the Eternal City.

I've clustered Rome's sights into walkable neighborhoods for more efficient sightseeing. In the Ancient Rome neighborhood, for example, you could string together a number of great sights, from the Colosseum to Capitoline Hill, in one sweaty day of sightseeing. For restaurant recommendations in these neighborhoods, ✪ see the maps on pages 179-182. For general sightseeing tips (reservations for the Colosseum, Vatican Museums, or Borghese Gallery, and more) see page 195.

Note that some of Rome's biggest sights (marked with a ✪) are described in more detail in the individual walks and tours chapters.

ANCIENT ROME

The core of the ancient city, where the grandest monuments were built, stretches from the Colosseum to Capitoline Hill. In Caesar's day, this was "downtown Rome"—citizens shopped at the bustling malls of the Forum, razzed gladiators at the Colosseum, and climbed Capitoline Hill to sacrifice a goat to Jupiter.

Today, the area is a rather barren tourist zone in the middle of the modern city. You'll find acres and acres of the planet's most famous ruins, but relatively few shops, restaurants, or everyday Romans. Fortunately, the modern world is just a few minutes' walk away. Metro stop Colosseo puts you right in the thick of the action. For eateries in the area, ✪ see page 177.

▲▲▲Colosseum (Colosseo)

The Colosseum, both in size and purpose, is the iconic symbol of the Roman Empire. Fifty thousand fans would pack this huge stadium and cheer for their favorite gladiators in bloody battles to the death. Today, visitors can go inside and bring that ancient world to life.

✪ See the Colosseum Tour on page 13.

▲▲▲Roman Forum (Foro Romano)

This is ancient Rome's birthplace and civic center, and the common ground between Rome's famous seven hills. For nearly a thousand years, the Forum was the heart of downtown Rome.

✪ See the Roman Forum Tour on page 27.

▲▲Palatine Hill (Monte Palatino)

The hill overlooking the Forum is jam-packed with history, but there's only the barest skeleton of rubble left to tell the story.

We get our word "palace" from this hill where the emperors lived in a sprawling 150,000-square-foot palace. You'll wander among vague outlines of rooms, courtyards, fountains, a banquet hall with a heated floor, and a sunken stadium. The throne room was the center of power for an empire of 50 million that stretched from England to Africa. The Palatine museum's statues and frescoes help you imagine the former luxury of this now-desolate hilltop. In one direction are expansive views over the dusty Circus Maximus chariot course. In the other are photogenic views of the Forum.

Sights

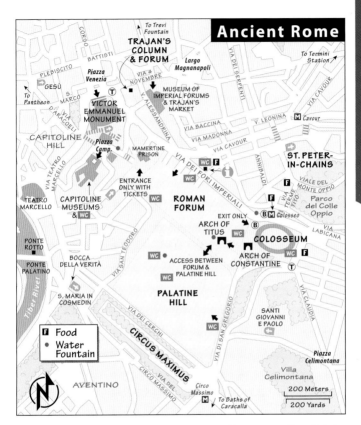

Ancient Rome

Supposedly, Romulus and Remus were suckled by a she-wolf on Palatine Hill, raised by shepherds, and grew to found the city in 753 B.C. Quaint legend? Well, here on Palatine Hill, you can see the remains of shepherds' huts, dated around 850 B.C. The legend enters into history.

► €12 combo-ticket includes the Roman Forum and Colosseum (after 14:00). Open daily 8:30 until one hour before sunset (✪ see page 28 for specific times); last entry one hour before closing.

The main entrance is 150 yards south of the Colosseum on Via di San

Gregorio. Consider buying your combo-ticket here, where there's rarely a line. You can also enter the Palatine from within the Roman Forum, near the Arch of Titus. WCs are at the main entrance, in the museum, near the stadium, and in the Farnese Gardens. Metro: Colosseo. Tel. 06-3996-7700.

▲Circus Maximus

Ancient Rome's most popular chariot-racing stadium was 2,100 feet long and could seat a quarter of a million spectators. Ben Hur-types raced around the central spine for seven thrilling laps while thousands cheered and placed bets on the outcome. Today, only a scant outline remains, but the sunken, cigar-shaped track has provided a natural amphitheater for concerts and public spectacles.

▶ *The Circus Maximus is always open and free. Metro: Circo Massimo.*

▲St. Peter-in-Chains Church (San Pietro in Vincoli)

Built in the fifth century to house the chains that held St. Peter (now under the altar), this church is most famous for Michelangelo's statue of Moses, intended for the tomb of Pope Julius II.

In 1505, the egomaniacal Pope Julius II asked Michelangelo to build a massive tomb—a free-standing pyramid, with 40 statues, to stand in the center of St. Peter's Basilica. Michelangelo labored on it for four decades, but got distracted by other gigs such as the Sistine Chapel. In 1542, Michelangelo and his assistants half heartedly pieced together a few remnants in St. Peter-in-Chains.

What we see today is not a full-blown 3-D pyramid but a 2-D wall monument framing a handful of statues. A statue of Pope Julius reclines on his fake coffin midway up the wall and looks down at the monument's highlight—Moses.

Moses, just returned from meeting face-to-face with God, senses trouble. Slowly he turns to see his followers worshipping a golden calf. As his anger builds, he glares and cradles the Ten Commandments, about to spring out of his chair and spank the naughty Children of Israel.

Why does Moses have horns? Centuries ago, the Hebrew word for "rays" was mistranslated as "horns." But it also captures an air of *terribilità,* a kind of scary charisma possessed by Moses, Pope Julius…and Michelangelo.

▶ *Free. Daily April-Sept 8:00-12:20 & 15:00-19:00, Oct-March until 18:00,*

Michelangelo's *Moses* at St. Peter-in-Chains   Trajan's Column and Forum

modest dress required. From the Colosseum, the church is a 15-minute uphill, zigzag walk. From the Cavour Metro station, walk downhill on Via Cavour a half-block, and then climb the pedestrian staircase.

Bocca della Verità

The "Mouth of Truth" at the Church of Santa Maria in Cosmedin draws a playful crowd. Stick your hand in the mouth of the gaping stone face in the porch wall. As the legend goes (popularized by the 1953 film *Roman Holiday*, starring Gregory Peck and Audrey Hepburn), if you're a liar, your hand will be gobbled up.

▶ *€2. Open daily 9:30-17:50, closes earlier off-season. At Piazza Bocca della Verità 18, near the north end of Circus Maximus, tel. 06-678-7759.*

▲▲Trajan's Column, Market, and Imperial Forums

Trajan's 140-foot column—the grandest from antiquity—was the center-piece of a complex of buildings built by the Emperor Trajan (who ruled A.D. 98-117). After Trajan conquered and looted central Europe, he returned to Rome with his booty and shook it all over the city. He built a forum of markets, civic buildings, and temples to rival the nearby Roman Forum.

Trajan's Column is carved with a spiral relief trumpeting Trajan's exploits. It winds upward—more than 200 yards long with 2,500 fig-ures—from the assembling of the army to the victory sacrifice at the top. A gleaming bronze statue of Trajan once capped the column, where St. Peter stands today.

The rest of Trajan's Forum is now ruined and a bit underwhelming, except for one grand structure—**Trajan's Market,** a semicircular brick building nestled into the cutaway curve of Quirinal Hill. Part shopping mall, part warehouse, part office building, this was where Romans could browse through goods from every corner of their vast empire—exotic fruits from Africa, spices from Asia, and fish-and-chips from Londinium. The 13 arches of the lower level may have held produce; the 26 windows above lit a covered arcade; and the roofline housed more stalls—150 shops in all.

The nearby **Museum of the Imperial Forums** has statue fragments and exhibits from both Trajan's Forum and the other forums that once stretched in a line along today's Via dei Fori Imperiali. The museum also gives you access to viewpoints atop Trajan's Market.

Appreciate Trajan's ambition. To build all this, he removed a natural ridgeline that once connected Capitoline Hill and Quirinal Hill. Trajan's Column marks the ridge's original height—140 feet.

▶ *Trajan's Column, Forum, and Market (always free and viewable) are just a few steps off Piazza Venezia, near the Victor Emmanuel Monument.*

The Museum of the Imperial Forums is at Via IV Novembre 94, up the staircase from Trajan's Column. €11.50. Open daily 9:30-19:30, last entry one hour before closing. Tel. 06-0608, www.mercatiditraiano.it.

Capitoline Hill and Piazza Venezia

The geographical (if not spiritual) center of Rome, this area straddles the ancient and modern worlds. Capitoline Hill was ancient Rome's political center, and today is home to several distinguished sights. At the foot of the hill is modern Piazza Venezia, a vast, traffic-filled square where four major boulevards meet. Between the Hill and the Plazza squats the massive white Victor Emmanuel Monument, 20 stories tall.

From Piazza Venezia, get oriented by standing with your back to the monument. Look down Via del Corso, the city's main north-south axis, surrounded by Rome's classiest shopping district. In the 1930s, Benito Mussolini whipped up Italy's fascist fervor in Piazza Venezia from the balcony on the left (the less-grand one). Mussolini had Via dei Fori Imperiali built (to your right) to open up views of the Colosseum to impress his visiting friend, Adolf Hitler. Traffic on this once-noisy boulevard is a pleasant walk, since it now is closed to private vehicles—and, on Sundays and holidays, to all traffic.

▲Capitoline Hill

Of Rome's famous seven hills, this is the smallest, tallest, and most famous. As home of the ancient Temple of Jupiter—the king of the gods—the

Capitoline Hill & Piazza Venezia

S. APOSTOLI

Villa Colonna

↑ To Piazza del Popolo

VIA DEL CORSO

GALLERIA DORIA PAMPHILJ

VIA BATTISTI

VIA 4 NOVEMBRE

VIA 4 NOVEMBRE

Piazza Venezia
#64, 40

VIA PLEBISCITO

Largo Magnanapoli

VIA NAZIONALE

PALAZZO VENEZIA

MUSSOLINI'S BALCONY

Ⓑ #64, 85

TRAJAN'S COLUMN

MUSEUM OF IMPERIAL FORUMS & TRAJAN'S MARKET

Ⓣ

TRAJAN'S

VIA ALESSANDRINA

To Gesù & Pantheon

SAN MARCO

Ⓑ #64

ENTRANCE & EMIGRATION MUSEUM

VICTOR EMMANUEL MONUMENT

FORUM

Ⓣ

VIA D'ARACOELI

ROME FROM THE SKY ELEVATOR

CAFÉ

STA. MARIA ARACOELI

Ⓑ #85, 87, 118 & 186

CAESAR'S FORUM

VIA DEI FORI IMPERIALI

MICHELANGELOS GRAND STAIRCASE

PALAZZO NUOVO

STATUE ■ Piazza del Campidoglio

DRINKING FOUNTAIN

To Colosseum & Ⓜ

Piazza Caffarelli

PUBLIC CAFÉ ENTRANCE

PALAZZO SENATORIO

SANTI LUCA E MARTINA

VIA TEATRO MARCELLO

CAPITOLINE MUSEUMS PALAZZO DEI CONSERVATORI

TABULARIUM

EXIT

ARCH OF SEPTIMIUS SEVERUS

ROMAN FORUM

CAFFÉ CAPITOLINO

FORO ROMANO

Ⓝ

100 Meters

100 Yards

Piazza d. Consolazione

hill was the seat of government, giving us our word "capitol." Some 2,500 years later, Rome is still ruled from here.

There are several routes to the top: From the Forum, take the steep staircase near the Arch of Septimius Severus. From Via dei Fori Imperiali, take the winding road. The grandest ascent is up the Michelangelo-built staircase from Piazza Venezia, to the right of the Victor Emmanuel Monument.

The square atop the hill—**Piazza del Campidoglio** (kahm-pi-DOHL-yoh)—resonates with history. In the 1530s, Michelangelo was asked to restore the square to its ancient glory. He placed the ancient equestrian statue of Marcus Aurelius as the square's focal point. Behind the statue he put the mayoral palace. The twin buildings on either side (now the Capitoline Museums) angle inward, drawing the visitor into this welcoming space. Michelangelo gave the buildings the "giant order"—tall pilasters that span two stories—making these big buildings feel more intimate.

The hill-topping **Santa Maria in Aracoeli** church houses a much-loved wooden statue (actually a copy) of the Baby Jesus (Santo Bambino) which locals venerate at Christmastime. The daunting 125-step staircase up to the church's front door was once climbed—on their knees—by Roman women who wished for a child. Today, they don't...and Italy has Europe's lowest birthrate.

▶ *The Campidoglio square is always open and free. The Santa Maria in Aracoeli church is open daily May-Sept 9:00-18:30, shorter hours off-season.*

Piazza del Campidoglio atop Capitoline Hill   A sliver of the vast Capitoline Museums

▲▲▲Capitoline Museums (Musei Capitolini)

Some of ancient Rome's most instantly recognizable statues are housed in the two palaces that flank the equestrian statue on Capitoline Hill.

In the Conservatori wing, you'll see the original statue of the she-wolf suckling the twins Romulus and Remus. This is the oldest known statue of this symbol of ancient Rome. Also in the museum is the original statue of Marcus Aurelius (the one in the Campidoglio is a copy), the greatest surviving equestrian statue of antiquity. Marcus was both an emperor (ruled A.D. 161-180) and a philosopher.

A bust of *Emperor Commodus as Hercules* depicts Marcus's bratty son. Commodus (ruled A.D. 180-192) earned a reputation for cruelty, dressing up like a demi-god and beating innocent people to death with his Hercules club. The well-known *Boy Extracting a Thorn* depicts one of those mundane moments in life when we'd give anything for tweezers.

In the Nuovo wing, the *Dying Gaul* (a first-century B.C. copy of a Greek original) shows a warrior wounded in battle. He holds himself upright, but barely, watching helplessly as his life ebbs away.

The museum also displays the scant remains of Capitoline Hill's once-massive, renowned Temple of Jupiter. Don't miss the Tabularium, the ancient Roman archive, which offers a superb view of the Forum.

▶ *€15. Open daily 9:30-19:30, last entry one hour before closing. The café has great city views. Tel. 06-0608, www.museicapitolini.org.*

▲Victor Emmanuel Monument

This oversized monument to Italy's first king was built to celebrate the 50th anniversary of the country's unification in 1861. Remember, after the fall of ancient Rome (A.D. 476), there was no Italian nation for over a thousand years. The Italian peninsula was a patchwork of bickering principalities and dukedoms dominated by foreigners. When Italy finally unified, this "Altar of the Nation" was a way to forge a new national identity through symbolism. Near the base, soldiers guard Italy's Tomb of the Unknown Soldier as Italian flags fly and the eternal flame flickers.

The gleaming white monument's scale is over the top: 200 feet high, 500 feet wide. The 43-foot-long statue of the king on his high horse is one of the biggest equestrian statues in the world. The king's moustache is five feet wide, and a person could sit within the horse's hoof. Atop the structure stand glorious chariots like on an ancient triumphal arch.

Locals love to hate the monument. It's been called "the wedding cake," "the typewriter," and "the dentures." (Most Romans just refer to it as "the Vittoriano.") It wouldn't be so bad if it weren't sitting on a priceless acre of ancient Rome.

You can climb the 242 punishing steps (or take the shortcut; see sidebar) to a middle level with great views of the Eternal City. From there, you can catch the **Rome from the Sky** elevator up to the tippy-top for a truly spectacular, 360-degree view—perhaps even better than from St. Peter's dome. Go in late afternoon, when it's beginning to cool off and Rome glows.

▶ *Daily 9:00 to 17:30, 9:30-16:30 in winter. WCs inside the monument. The Rome from the Sky elevator costs €7 and runs daily until 19:30, ticket office closes 45 minutes earlier, tel. 06-679-3598. Catch it near the top, by the outdoor café, following signs to* ascensori panoramici.

Locals love to hate the grandiose Victor Emmanuel Monument, but the view from the top is fantastic.

PANTHEON NEIGHBORHOOD

The area around the Pantheon is the heart of Rome. Here, you see all of the city's historic layers on display—ancient ruins, medieval lanes, Baroque fountains, and modern Romans at work and play. This neighborhood stretches from the Tiber River through Campo de' Fiori and Piazza Navona, past the Pantheon to the Trevi Fountain. To get here by taxi or bus (#64 or #40), aim for the large square called Largo Argentina, a few blocks south of the Pantheon.

Besides being home to ancient sights and historic churches, the Pantheon neighborhood gives Rome its urban-village feel. Wander narrow streets, sample the many shops and eateries, and gather with the locals in squares marked by bubbling fountains. It's especially enjoyable in the

evening, with a gelato in hand, when restaurants bustle and streets are jammed with foot traffic.

For area restaurants, ✪ see page 173. For a good introductory walk through the neighborhood, ✪ see the Heart of Rome Walk on page 43.

▲▲▲The Pantheon

If your imagination is fried from trying to reconstruct ancient buildings out of today's rubble, visit the Pantheon, Rome's best-preserved monument. Engineers still admire how the Romans built such a mathematically precise structure without computers, fossil-fuel-run machinery, or electricity. (Having unlimited slave power didn't hurt.)

Exterior: The Pantheon was a Roman temple dedicated to all (pan) of the gods *(theos),* a one-stop-shopping temple where you could worship any of the gods whose statues decorated the niches. The original temple was built in 27 B.C. by Emperor Augustus' son-in-law, Marcus Agrippa (as the Latin inscription above the columns proclaims). The structure we see today dates from around A.D. 120, built by Emperor Hadrian. The 40-foot-high columns were taken from an Egyptian temple.

Interior—The Dome: The awe-inspiring dome is mathematically

The Pantheon dome rises from thick walls at the base, to thin at the top, to the open-air oculus.

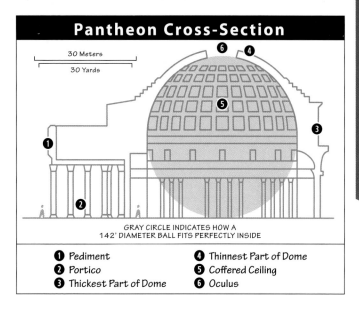

Pantheon Cross-Section

30 Meters

30 Yards

❶ Pediment
❷ Portico
❸ Thickest Part of Dome
❹ Thinnest Part of Dome
❺ Coffered Ceiling
❻ Oculus

GRAY CIRCLE INDICATES HOW A
142' DIAMETER BALL FITS PERFECTLY INSIDE

perfect: 142 feet tall and 142 feet wide. It rests atop a circular base; imagine a basketball set inside a wastebasket so that it just touches bottom. The dome is constructed from concrete, a Roman invention. The base is 23 feet thick and made from heavy travertine concrete, while the top is five feet thick and made from light volcanic pumice. The square indentations (or coffers) reduce the weight of the dome without compromising strength. At the top, the **oculus,** or eye-in-the-sky, is the building's only light source and is almost 30 feet across. The Pantheon also contains the world's greatest Roman column—the pillar of light from the oculus.

This dome is perhaps the most influential in art history. It inspired Brunelleschi's Florence cathedral dome, Michelangelo's dome of St. Peter's, and even the capitol dome of Washington, DC.

The Rest: The marble floor—with its design of alternating circles and squares—is largely original. It has holes in it and slants toward the edges to let the rainwater drain.

Early in the Middle Ages, the Pantheon became a Christian church

The Pantheon—Rome's best-preserved temple   Caravaggio masterpiece at San Luigi church

(from "all the gods" to "all the martyrs"), which means it's been in continual use for nearly 1,900 years. To the right of the altar is the tomb of Italy's first modern king, Victor Emmanuel II (*"Padre della Patria,"* father of the fatherland), and to the left is Umberto I (son of the father). Also to the left of the altar, the artist Raphael lies buried, in a lighted glass niche.

▶ *Usually free but may require a €2 ticket. Open Mon-Sat 8:30-19:30, Sun 9:00-18:00, holidays 9:00-13:00, closed for Mass on Sat at 17:00 and Sun at 10:30. Tel. 06-6830-0230. No skimpy shorts or bare shoulders. Photography is allowed. A free ∩ Rick Steves audio tour is available (✪ see page 195). The Pantheon is north of Largo Argentina, a major transportation hub for taxis and buses #40 and #64.*

▲▲Campo de' Fiori

One of Rome's most colorful spots, this bohemian piazza hosts a fruit-and-vegetable market in the morning, cafés in the evening, and pub crawlers at night.

✪ See page 44 in the Heart of Rome Walk chapter.

▲▲Piazza Navona

This long, oval-shaped piazza—dotted with fountains and surrounded by open-air restaurants—attracts both locals and tourists, especially at night.

✪ See page 45 in the Heart of Rome Walk chapter.

▲▲Church of San Luigi dei Francesi

The French national church in Rome has one truly magnifique sight—the chapel in the far left corner, decorated by the groundbreaking Baroque painter Caravaggio (1571-1610).

In *The Calling of St. Matthew* (left wall), Jesus walks into a dingy bar, raises his arm, and points to a sheepish Matthew, calling him to discipleship. The other two paintings show where Matthew's call led him—writing a Gospel of Jesus' life (center wall), and eventually giving up his own life for the Christian cause (*Martyrdom,* right).

Caravaggio shocked the religious world by showing holy scenes with gritty, ultra-realistic details—a balding saint, an angel that doesn't glow, a truly scary executioner—all lit by a harsh third-degree spotlight that pierces the gloom. In the *Martyrdom,* the bearded face in the background (to the left of the executioner's shoulder) is a self-portrait of a dispassionate Caravaggio.

▶ *Free. Open daily 9:30-12:30 & 14:30-18:30 except opens Sun at 10:30, www.saintlouis-rome.net. Bring coins to light the Caravaggios.*

▲▲Gesù Church

The center of the Jesuit order and the best symbol of the Catholic Counter-Reformation, the Gesù (jay-zoo) is packed with overblown art and underappreciated history. The facade's scroll-like shoulders became the model for hundreds of similar Catholic churches across the globe, signaling the coming of Baroque.

Inside, the huge ceiling fresco (by Il Baciccio) shows a glowing cross with the Jesuit seal ("I.H.S."). The cross astounds the faithful and sends infidels plunging downward. The damned spill over the edge of the painting's frame, becoming 3-D stucco sculptures, on their way to hell. As Catholics fought Protestants for the hearts and minds of the world's Christians, this propaganda art had a clear message—pervert the true faith, and this is your fate.

The founder of the Jesuit order, St. Ignatius of Loyola (1491-1556), lies buried in the left transept beneath a towering altarpiece. Ignatius, a war veteran wounded in battle, rallied Jesuit monks to be ideological warriors, fighting heretics such as Martin Luther. To the right of the altarpiece, a statue shows the Church as an angry nun hauling back with a whip and just spanking a bunch of miserable Protestants. Not too subtle.

▶ *Free. Open daily 7:00-12:30 & 16:00-19:45. The multimedia 17:30 service highlights Ingnatius' tomb. Tel. 06-697-001, www.chiesadelgesu.org.*

▲▲Church of Santa Maria sopra Minerva

This church is a mishmash of minor sights. From the outside, see an Egyptian obelisk atop a Baroque elephant (by Bernini) in front of a Gothic church built over *(sopra)* a pagan Temple of Minerva. Inside Rome's only Gothic church, you'll see crisscross arches, a starry ceiling, and stained-glass windows. Under the main altar lies the body of St. Catherine of Siena (her head is in Siena). In the 1300s, this Italian nun was renowned for having visions of her mystical marriage with Jesus.

Left of the altar stands Michelangelo's statue of *Christ Bearing the Cross* (1519-1520). His athletic body, bulging biceps, awkwardly posed legs—and the fact that the statue was completed by a mediocre assistant—made this one of the master's less-renowned works.

The tomb of Fra Angelico ("Beato Angelico 1387-1455"), the great early Renaissance painter and Dominican monk, is near the statue, just up the three stairs.

▶ *Free. Open Mon-Fri 7:30-19:00, Sat-Sun 8:00-12:30 & 15:30-19:00, www.santamariasopraminerva.it.*

Church of Sant'Ignazio

The interior décor is a riot of Baroque illusions. The colorful ceiling fresco shows St. Ignatius having a vision of Christ with the Cross. The cross radiates heavenly light to the four corners of the earth—including America (to the left), depicted as a bare-breasted Native American maiden spearing naked men. Note how the actual columns of the church are extended into the painting. Now fix your eyes on the arch at the far end of the painting. Walk up the nave, and watch the arch grow and tower over you.

Before you reach the center of the church, stop at the small yellow disk on the floor and look up into the central (black) dome. Keeping your eye on the dome, walk under and past it. Building project runs out of money? Hire a painter to paint a fake, flat dome.

Back outside, the church stands on a square with several converging streets that has been compared to a stage set. Sit on the church steps, admire the theatrical yellow backdrop of the building across the way, and watch the "actors" enter one way and exit another, in the human opera that is modern Rome.

▶ *Free. Open Mon-Sat 7:30-19:00, Sun 9:00-19:00, www.chiesasantignazio. it.*

▲Galleria Doria Pamphilj

This underappreciated gallery, tucked away in the heart of the old city, offers a rare chance to wander through a noble family's lavish mansion crammed with world-class art. The audioguide (included) is lovingly narrated by the current prince.

Don't miss Velázquez's intense, majestic, ultra-realistic portrait of the family founder, Pope Innocent X. It stands alongside an equally impressive bust of the pope by the father of the Baroque art style, Gian Lorenzo Bernini. Stroll through a mini-Versailles-like hall of mirrors to more paintings, including works by Titian and Raphael. Finally, relax along with Mary, Joseph, and Jesus, and let the angel serenade you in Caravaggio's *Rest on the Flight to Egypt.*

▸ *€12. Open daily 9:00-19:00, last entry one hour before closing, elegant café. Located two blocks north of Piazza Venezia at Via del Corso 305. Tel. 06-679-7323, www.dopart.it/roma.*

▲Trevi Fountain

The bubbly Baroque fountain—worth ▲▲ by night—is a minor sight to art scholars but a major gathering spot for teens on the make and tourists tossing coins.

✪ See page 50 in the Heart of Rome Walk chapter.

NEAR TERMINI TRAIN STATION

While the train station neighborhood is not atmospheric, it contains some high-powered sights. These sights are within a 10-minute walk of the station, near Metro stops Termini and Repubblica.

▲▲▲National Museum of Rome
(Museo Nazionale Romano Palazzo Massimo alle Terme)

Rome lasted a thousand years...and so do most Roman history courses. But if you want a breezy overview of this fascinating society, there's no better place than the National Museum of Rome. The National Museum's main branch, at Palazzo Massimo, houses the greatest collection of ancient Roman art anywhere.

On the ground floor, gaze eye-to-eye with the busts of famous Romans. There's Julius Caesar, who conquered Gaul, impregnated

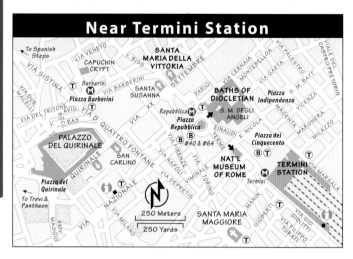

Near Termini Station

Cleopatra, and created one-man rule. His adopted son Augustus, shown wearing the hooded robes of a priest, became the first emperor. The rest of the Julio-Claudian family is a parade of shady characters—Augustus' wily wife Livia, her moody son Tiberius, and crazy Caligula, who ordered men to kneel before him as a god.

The statue of the *Boxer at Rest* shows an exhausted pugilist slumped between rounds, gasping for air. His face is scarred, his back muscles are knotted, and his hollow-eyed expression says, "I coulda been a contender."

On the first floor is the best-preserved Roman copy of the Greek *Discus Thrower.* Caught in mid-motion, his perfect balance summed up the order the ancients saw in nature. Statues of athletes like this commonly stood in the baths, where Romans cultivated healthy bodies, minds, and social skills, hoping to lead well-rounded lives.

The second floor focuses on frescoes and mosaics that once decorated the walls and floors of Roman villas. The basement has the best coin collection in Europe, from the ancient Roman denar to the Italian lira.

▶ *€10. Open Tue-Sun 9:00-19:45, closed Mon, last entry one hour before closing. Located 100 yards from the train station. Metro: Repubblica or Termini, tel. 06-3996-7700, www.museonazionaleromano. benicultural.it.*

▲Baths of Diocletian (Terme di Diocleziano) at Santa Maria degli Angeli

Around A.D. 300, Emperor Diocletian built the largest baths in Rome—a sprawling complex of pools, gyms, and schmoozing spaces that could accommodate 3,000 bathers at a time. While most of it is ruined, a few sections have been incorporated into the Church of Santa Maria degli Angeli.

The church entrance (on noisy Piazza della Repubblica) is where the baths' *caldarium* once stood, the steam room where Romans worked up a sweat. Next, they'd step into the cooler *tepidarium* (now the domed entry hall of the church), where masseuses rubbed them down.

Continue into what was once the baths' huge central hall—a football field long and seven stories high. The eight red granite columns and crisscross arches on the ceiling are original. Beyond today's church altar was the *frigidarium,* with a 32,000-square-foot swimming pool. Mentally undress your fellow tourists and imagine hundreds of ancient Romans milling about, wrestling, doing jumping jacks, singing in the baths, and networking. Shops, bars, and fast-food vendors once catered to every Roman need.

The church we see today (from 1561) was partly designed by Michelangelo, who used the baths' main hall as the church's nave.

On the floor is a meridian (from 1702), a line that points north and acts as a sundial and calendar. A ray of light enters the church through a tiny hole 65 feet up the wall of the right transept. The light sweeps across the meridian at exactly noon. Where the ray crosses the line tells you the date.

The Baths of Diocletian functioned until A.D. 537, when barbarians cut the city's aqueducts, plunging Rome into a thousand years of poverty, darkness, and B.O.

Boxer at Rest at the National Museum

St. Teresa at Santa Maria della Vittoria

▶ *Free. Open Mon-Sat 7:00-18:30, Sun until 19:30, closed to sightseers during Mass. Entrance on Piazza della Repubblica, Metro: Repubblica.*

▲Santa Maria della Vittoria

This small church houses Gian Lorenzo Bernini's best-known statue, the swooning *St. Teresa in Ecstasy* (1652).

Teresa has just been stabbed with God's arrow of fire. Now, the angel pulls it out and watches her reaction. Teresa swoons, her eyes roll up, her hand goes limp, she parts her lips...and moans. The smiling, cherubic angel understands just how she feels. Teresa, a 16th-century Spanish nun, later talked of the "sweetness" of "this intense pain," describing her oneness with God in ecstatic, even erotic, terms.

Bernini (1598-1680), the master of multimedia, pulls out all the stops to make this mystical vision real. Actual sunlight pours through the alabaster windows, and bronze sunbeams shine on a marble angel holding a golden arrow. Teresa leans back on a cloud and her robe ripples from within, charged with her spiritual arousal. Bernini has created a little stage-setting of heaven. And watching from the "theater boxes" on either side are members of the family that commissioned the work.

▶ *Free, but bring €0.50 for coin-op light. Open Mon-Sat 8:30-12:00 & 15:30-18:00, Sun 15:30-18:00. Located 5 blocks northwest of Termini train station at Via XX Settembre 17, Metro: Repubblica.*

NORTH ROME

The Villa Borghese Gardens form the northern border of tourists' Rome. Several sights lie inside the landscaped park, while others ring its southern perimeter, clustered around the Spanish Steps, Via Veneto, and Piazza del Popolo. The area has some of Rome's classiest fashion boutiques. Metro stops Spagna, Barberini, and Flaminio serve the neighborhood. For recommended restaurants in the area, ✪ see page 174.

▲▲▲Borghese Gallery (Galleria Borghese)

This plush museum, filling a cardinal's mansion in the park, offers one of Europe's most sumptuous art experiences. You'll enjoy theatrical statues by Bernini and paintings by Caravaggio, Raphael, and others.

✪ See the Borghese Gallery Tour chapter on page 105.

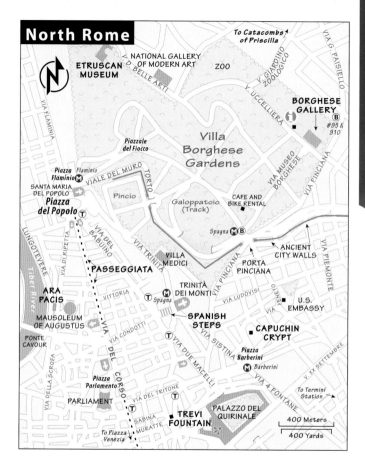

Villa Borghese Gardens

Rome's scruffy, three-square-mile "Central Park" is great for its shade and for people-watching the city's modern-day Romeos and Juliets. The best entrance is at the head of Via Veneto. (From Metro Barberini, walk 10 minutes up Via Veneto and through the old Roman wall at Porta Pinciana.

Metro stop Spagna is equally close, but the route is circuitous.) There you'll find a cluster of buildings with a café, a kiddie arcade, and bike rental (€4/hour). Rent a bike, or, for romantics, a pedaled rickshaw *(riscio)*. Follow signs to discover the park's cafés, fountains, statues, lake, viewpoint over Piazza del Popolo, and prime picnic spots.

Of the park's several museums, consider the **Etruscan Museum.** The fascinating Etruscan civilization thrived in central Italy around 600 B.C., back when Rome was just another Etruscan town. The museum's highlight is the famous "husband and wife sarcophagus." The elegant couple reclines atop their tomb (sixth century B.C., from Cerveteri), seeming to enjoy an everlasting banquet.

▶ *Museum is €8. Open Tue-Sun 8:30-19:30, closed Mon, last entry one hour before closing, scant English information. It's a 20-minute walk from the Borghese Gallery or most Villa Borghese Garden entrances at Piazzale di Villa Giulia 9, tel. 06-322-6571, www.villagiulia.beniculturali.it.*

▲Capuchin Crypt (Cripta dei Frati Cappuccini)

If you want to see artistically arranged bones in Italy, this is the place. The skulls, femurs, and tibias of 4,000 friars who died between 1528 and 1870 line the walls and ceilings in intricate patterns, to the delight—or disgust—of the always-wide-eyed visitor. As you enter, a monastic message on the wall reminds you: "We were what you are...you will become what we are now."

Your visit starts in a museum about the Capuchin order; then you descend to the crypt, where each of six small chapels has its own theme. The Crypt of the Three Skeletons is about the Day of Judgment. A skeleton on the ceiling wields a grim-reaper scythe and a set of scales to weigh souls. The chapel's bony chandelier and floral motifs made from ribs and vertebrae are particularly inspired. In another chapel, an hourglass with wings reminds us that, yes, time on Earth flies. You'll see a jaunty skull with a shoulder-blade bowtie, a canopy of hipbones with vertebrae bangles, and robed skeletons of Capuchin friars—the monks whose robes gave the name to the brown coffee with the frothy white cowl. One chapel has a floor of dirt brought from Jerusalem, and 18 graves. As you leave (humming, "The foot bone's connected to the..."), pick up a few of Rome's most interesting postcards.

▶ *€8.50. Open daily 9:00-19:00. Modest dress is required, no photos.*

Capuchin Crypt—dem bones, dem bones…   Ara Pacis—once-bloody sacrificial altar

Located at Via Veneto 27, just up from Metro: Barberini. Tel. 06-8880-3695, www.cappucciniviaveneto.it.

▲Spanish Steps

This picturesque staircase near a ritzy shopping area attracts people day and night. Like a mini-amphitheater, the staircase is the perfect spot for taking a seat and observing Roman life.

✪ See page 51 in the Heart of Rome Walk chapter.

▲▲Museo dell'Ara Pacis (Museum of the Altar of Peace)

On January 30, 9 B.C., soon-to-be-emperor Augustus led a procession of priests up the steps and into this newly built "Altar of Peace." They sacrificed an animal on the altar and poured an offering of wine, thanking the gods for helping Augustus pacify barbarians abroad and rivals at home. This marked the dawn of the Pax Romana (c. A.D. 1-200), a Golden Age of good living, stability, dominance, and peace *(pax)*.

Though simple, the Ara Pacis (AH-rah PAH-chees) has all the essentials of a Roman temple: an altar for sacrifices surrounded by cubicle-like walls that enclose a consecrated space. At the base of the walls, you can still see the drain holes for washing the blood out.

The reliefs on the north side depict the parade of dignitaries who consecrated the altar. Augustus stands near the head (his body sliced in two vertically by missing stone), honored with a crown of laurel leaves. He's followed by a half-dozen bigwigs and priests (with spiked hats) and the man shouldering the sacrificial axe. Reliefs on the west side (near the altar's back door) celebrate Augustus' major accomplishments: peace (goddess Roma as a conquering Amazon, right side) and prosperity (fertility goddess). Imagine the altar as it once was, standing in an open field, painted in bright colors—a mingling of myth, man, and nature.

▶ *€10.50; tightwads can look in through huge windows for free. Good €4 audioguide. Open daily 9:30-19:30, last entry one hour before closing. Located on the east bank of the Tiber, on Via di Ara Pacis. From the Spanish Steps (Metro: Spagna) it's a 10-minute walk down Via dei Condotti. Tel. 06-0608, www.arapacis.it.*

Via del Corso Passeggiata

Every evening, Rome's main north-south street closes to car traffic for a few hours (roughly 17:00-19:00), and Romans flood the streets for a classic ritual found in almost every Italian town—the *passeggiata,* or evening stroll. Shoppers, people-watchers, and dressed-up older folks mingle with young flirts on the prowl. It's a time to get out of the house after the heat of the afternoon, greet neighbors, show off your latest outfit, and check out your gender of choice. This neighborhood has some of Rome's most fashionable stores (generally open until 19:30), and many bars host happy hours. Saturdays and Sundays bring out the most festive crowds.

Start on Piazza del Popolo (Metro: Flaminio). This vast oval square marks the traditional north entrance to Rome. From here, three roads head south from the piazza, forming the shape of a trident (the Tridente), and leading to the city center. Head down Via del Corso.

Observe the flirtation. You may hear genteel whispers of *"bella"* and *"bello"* ("pretty" and "handsome"), as well as cruder language—*"buona"* and *"buono,"* meaning roughly "tasty."

End your walk at Piazza Venezia for great sunset views from atop Capitoline Hill. Or turn left at Via Condotti, window-shopping your way past trendy boutiques to the Spanish Steps (Metro: Spagna).

▲▲Catacombs of Priscilla (Catacombe di Priscilla)

While most tourists flock to the more famous catacombs on the ancient Appian Way, these are less commercialized and crowded, and feel more intimate.

These catacombs began as underground tombs for early Christians who once worshipped in a home on this spot. You enter from a convent and explore a honeycomb of tunnels dug between the second and fifth centuries. You'll see some of the 40,000 burial niches carved into the

Sights

volcanic tuff stone, along with a few beautiful frescoes, including what is considered the first depiction of Mary nursing the baby Jesus.

▶ *€8. Open Tue-Sun 9:00-12:00 & 14:00-17:00, closed Mon, closed one random month a year—check website or call first Via Salaria 430. Tel. 06-8620-6272, www.catacombepriscilla.com. Visits are by 30-minute guided tour only (English-language tours depart generally every 20 minutes).*

The catacombs are on the northeast edge of the city but well-served by direct buses (30 minutes from Termini or 40 minutes from Piazza Venezia) or a €15 taxi ride—tell the cabbie "Piazza Crati" and mention the "kah-ta-KOHM-bay." From Termini, take bus #92 or #310 from Piazza Cinquecento. From Piazza Venezia, along Via del Corso or Via Barberini, take bus #63 or #83. Located at Via Salaria 430.

VATICAN CITY AND NEARBY

Vatican City contains the Vatican Museums (with Michelangelo's Sistine Chapel) and St. Peter's Basilica (with Michelangelo's exquisite *Pietà*). It sits on the west bank of the Tiber in an otherwise nondescript neighborhood. Nearby are a few lesser sights. Metro stops Ottaviano and Cipro are handy, and buses #64 and #40 stop in the area. For restaurant recommendations, ✪ see page 175.

▲▲▲Vatican Museums (Musei Vaticani)

The four miles of displays in this immense museum complex—from ancient statues to Christian frescoes to modern paintings—culminate in the Raphael Rooms and Michelangelo's glorious Sistine Chapel.

✪ See the Vatican Museums Tour chapter on page 53.

▲▲▲St. Peter's Basilica (Basilica San Pietro)

The richest and grandest church on earth has a long history and several major sights, including Michelangelo's *Pietà* and a dome with great views of Rome.

✪ See the St. Peter's Basilica Tour chapter on page 81.

▲Castel Sant'Angelo

This giant pile of ancient bricks is packed with history. Emperor Hadrian

Vatican City

TRIONFALE

Piazzale degli Eroi

VIA ANDREA DORIA

MERCATO TRIONFALE

VIALE GIULIO CESARE

To Ⓜ Cipro

VIA LEONE IV

VIA TUNISI

Ottaviano Ⓜ

VIA DEGLI SCIPIONI

Piazza dei Quiriti

Ⓑ #492

VIA CANDIA

VIA SEBASTIANO VENIERO

Ⓣ Ⓑ #49

VIA BARLETTA

VIA OTTAVIANO

VIA COLA DI RIENZO

V. ANGELO EMO

VAT. MUS. ENTRANCE Ⓣ Ⓑ

Ⓑ #492

Piazza Risorgimento

VIA CRESCENZIO

VIALE VATICANO

WALL

ITALIAN POST

VIA CONCILIAZIONE

CASTEL SANT' ANGELO

WALL

VATICAN MUSEUMS

BORGO VITTORIO

BORGO PIO

VATICAN CITY

Gardens

SISTINE CHAPEL

PAPAL APT.

VIA CORRIDORI

RADIO VATICAN

ST. PETER'S

St. Peter's Square

■ OBELISK

Ⓣ

#40 Ⓑ

VIA DELLA CONCILIAZIONE

BORGO SANTO SPIRITO

Tiber

WALL

ⓘ ■

AUDIENCE HALL

POST OFFICE & Ⓦ𝖢

PONTE VITTORIO EMANUELE II

Ⓑ #64

TUNNEL

200 Meters

200 Yards

V. PORTA CAVALLEGGERI

V. STAZIONE

To San Pietro Train Stn.

To Trastevere

PONTE PRINCIPE AMEDEO

designed it as his own tomb (C. A.D. 139)—a towering cylinder, 210 feet by 70 feet, topped by a cypress grove and crowned with a huge statue of Hadrian himself riding a chariot.

As Rome fell, the mausoleum became a fortress and prison. When the archangel Michael appeared miraculously above the structure (A.D. 590), the "castle" was renamed for this "holy angel." Through the centuries, it was expanded upward and connected to the Vatican via an elevated corridor (1277), making it a handy place of last refuge for threatened popes.

Touring the inside, you trudge 400 feet up a spiral ramp to where Hadrian's ashes were once placed. Next comes the medieval addition, decorated with papal splendor. Don't miss the Sala del Tesoro (Treasury), where the wealth of the Vatican was locked up in a huge chest. (*Do* miss

Castel Sant'Angelo—a former tomb   The *Scala Santa*—a sacred Stairmaster

the 58 rooms of the lackluster military museum.) Finally you emerge at the castle's highlight—the rooftop viewpoint—where you can survey the city like a pope or emperor.

▶ *€10. Open daily 9:00-19:30, last entry one hour before closing. Located along the Tiber, near Vatican City at Lungotevere Castello 50, Metro: Lepanto or bus #40 or #64. Tel. 06-681-9111, www.castelsantangelo. beniculturali.it.*

PILGRIM'S ROME

In eastern Rome lie several venerable churches that Catholic pilgrims make a point of visiting. The main sights are found within a triangle formed by Termini station, the Colosseum, and the San Giovanni Metro stop.

Rome is the "capital" of the world's 1.2 billion Catholics. Since ancient days, pilgrims have flocked to this city where Peter and Paul preached, where Christians were martyred, Constantine legalized the religion, miraculous relics were kept, and where the pope still reigns. It was the flood of pilgrims that shaped Rome's tourist industry. In your visit today, you'll rub elbows with Nigerian nuns, Bulgarian theology novices, students from Notre Dame, extended Mexican families, and everyday Catholics returning to their religious roots.

Church of San Giovanni in Laterano

When this church opened its doors in A.D. 318, it became the first place in Rome where once-persecuted Christians could finally "come out" and worship openly. Through medieval times, San Giovanni was home of the popes and the center of Catholicism until the new St. Peter's opened at the Vatican during the Renaissance.

Despite its history, the church is rather barren, having been redone in the 1600s. The spacious nave—a central hall flanked by side aisles—was the model for all basilicas to follow. The 2,000-year-old bronze doors originally hung at the ancient Senate House in the Forum. You'll see (supposed) relics of Peter and Paul and (supposed) bronze columns from the Temple of Jupiter. The bishop's chair (cathedra) reminds visitors that this (not St. Peter's) is the city's cathedral, presided over by the bishop of Rome—the pope.

▶ *Free. Open daily 7:00-18:30. The cloister (€5) has a Cosmati-designed mosaic floor. Metro: San Giovanni, or bus #87. Tel. 06-6988-6409, www.scalasantaroma.it.*

▲Holy Stairs (Scala Santa)

A building near the Church of San Giovanni in Laterano houses a staircase said to have been touched by Jesus. The 28 marble steps once stood in Pontius Pilate's residence in Jerusalem. Jesus climbed these steps on the day he was sentenced to death. In 326, Emperor Constantine's mother (Sta. Helena) brought them to Rome, where they were subsequently protected with a covering of walnut wood.

Each day, hundreds of faithful penitents climb these steps on their knees, reciting prayers. They look down through glass-covered sections to see stains from Jesus' blood. Visitors can join in or observe from the side. The steps lead to the "Holy of Holies" (Sancta Sanctorum), a chapel which, in medieval times, held important relics (now gone), and was once considered the holiest place on earth.

▶ *Free. Open Mon-Sat 6:30-19:00, Sun 7:00-19:00, Oct-March closes daily at 18:30. Metro: San Giovanni.*

Church of Santa Maria Maggiore

One of Rome's oldest (A.D. 432), simplest, and best-preserved churches, Santa Maria Maggiore was a rare oasis of order in the days when Rome was falling around it. The church is dedicated to Holy Mary, the mother of Christ, and pilgrims come to kneel before an urn containing pieces of wood from Jesus' manger (in a lighted niche under the altar). Some of Rome's best-surviving (if hard-to-see) mosaics line the nave (bring binoculars).

The church has a glorious altar of precious stones (left transept) as

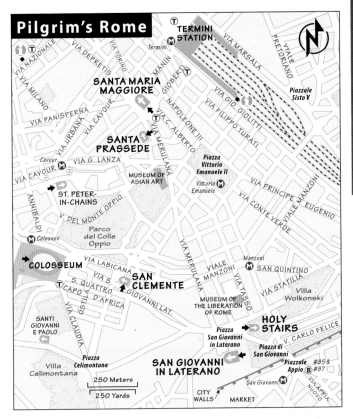

Pilgrim's Rome

well as the humble floor tomb of the artist Bernini (right of the altar). In the right transept is a monument to the man who rebuilt Rome in the 16th century, the energetic Pope Sixtus V. Or was it Fiftus VI?

▶ Free. Open daily 7:00-18:45. Metro: Termini or Vittorio Emanuele. Tel. 06-6988-6800.

Church of Santa Prassede

This church sparkles with ninth-century mosaics—a glimmer of light during

Rome's Dark Ages. The apse mosaic shows Christ (on a rainbow river) commanding Peter (white hair and beard) to convert pagan Rome. In the side chapel of St. Zeno, the gold ceiling represents heaven, with Christ supported by four angels in white.

▸ *Free. Open daily 7:00-12:00 & 15:00-18:30, no visit during Mass (Mon-Sat 7:30 & 18:00; Sun 8:00, 10:00, 11:30, and 18:00). 100 yards from Church of Santa Maria Maggiore on Via S. Giovanni Gualberto.*

▲Church of San Clemente

Here, like nowhere else, you'll enjoy the layers of Rome. A 12th-century basilica sits atop a fourth-century Christian basilica, which sits atop a second-century Mithraic temple and some even earlier Roman buildings.

On street level, you enter the 12th-century church, featuring original mosaics (in the apse) of Christ on the cross, surrounded by doves, animals, and a Tree of Life. The message: All life springs from God in Christ.

Next, descend to a fourth-century church. A faded fresco shows St. Clement holding a secret Mass for persecuted Christians, when he's suddenly arrested. As they try to drag him away (the Latin inscription reads), a man yells, *"Fili dele pute!... You sons of bitches!"*

Finally, descend one more floor, to the dark, dank remains of the pagan cult of Mithras. Worshippers—men only—huddled on the benches of this low-ceilinged room. The room was a microcosm of the universe—the ceiling was once covered with stars, and the small shafts let priests follow the movements of the heavens. A carved altar shows the god Mithras, in a billowing cape, running his sword through a sacred bull. The blood spills out, bringing life to the world. Mithras' fans gathered here to eat a ritual meal celebrating the triumph of light and life over darkness and death.

▸ *Upper church is free to visit, €10 for the lower levels. Open Mon-Sat 9:00-12:30 & 15:00-18:00, Sun 12:15-18:00. Entrance on Via di San Giovanni in Laterano, Metro: Colosseo. Tel. 06-774-0021, www. basilicasanclemente.com.*

TRASTEVERE AND NEARBY

Trastevere (trahs-TAY-veh-ray) is a colorful neighborhood with a medieval-village feel across (*tras*) the Tiber (*Tevere*) River. It's tucked into the bend in the river, near the island in the Tiber, surrounding the church of Santa Maria in Trastevere. There are no must-see tourist sights, but it's a great people scene, especially at night. Streets are narrow and tangled. The action unwinds to the chime of the church bells. This former working-class area is becoming trendy, but it's still as close to the "real Rome" as you can get. It's a great place for dinner—for restaurant recommendations, ✪ see pages 175-177. A free 🎧 Rick Steves audio tour of Trastevere is available (✪ see page 195).

To reach Trastevere by foot from Capitoline Hill, cross the Tiber on Ponte Cestio (over Isola Tiberina). You can also take tram #8 from Piazza Venezia, or bus #H from Termini and Piazza Repubblica to Piazza Belli. From the Vatican (Piazza Risorgimento), it's bus #23 or #271.

▲Church of Santa Maria in Trastevere

One of Rome's oldest churches, this was made a basilica in the fourth century, when Christianity was legalized. It is said to have been the first church in Rome dedicated to the Virgin Mary. Its portico (covered area just outside the door) is decorated with fascinating fragments of stone—many of them lids from catacomb burial niches—and filled with early Christian symbolism.

The piazza outside is the neighborhood meeting place, where kids play soccer, layabouts lay about the fountain steps, and people crowd the outdoor restaurants.

▶ *Free. Open daily 7:30-21:00, except Aug 8:00-12:00 & 16:00-21:00.*

▲Villa Farnesina

This sumptuous Renaissance villa decorated with Raphael paintings was built in the early 1500s for the richest man in Renaissance Europe, Sienese banker Agostino Chigi. It was a meeting place of aristocrats, artists, beautiful women, and philosophers, a place where art, nature, and ideas blended in harmony. Both Agostino and Raphael were notorious womanizers, and the decor drips with erotic themes.

The Loggia of Galatea has Raphael's famous painting of the nymph Galatea. She shuns the ungainly one-eyed giant Polyphemus and speeds away on a chariot led by dolphins. She turns back and looks up, amused by the cyclops' crude love song (which, I believe, was "I Only Have Eye for You").

In the Loggia of Psyche, Raphael's ceiling frescoes depict the myth of

Trastevere—a bit rougher but more real

The former Jewish ghetto has new life.

the lovely mortal woman, Psyche (in topless robe), who fell in love with the winged boy-god Cupid, or Eros.

Upstairs, you reach Agostino's small bedroom. The painting (by Il Sodoma) shows the wedding of Alexander the Great. His bride Roxanne has the features of Agostino's own bride, and the bed is the jewel-encrusted ebony bed that received Agostino and his beloved here on their wedding night.

▸ *€6. Open Mon-Sat 9:00-14:00, closed Sun except open 9:00-17:00 on second Sun of the month. Located near Ponte Sisto at Via della Lungara 230. Tel. 06-6802-7268, www.villafarnesina.it.*

▲Jewish Quarter

From the 16th through the 19th centuries, Rome's Jewish population was required to live in a cramped ghetto at an often-flooded bend of the Tiber River. While the medieval Jewish ghetto is long gone, this area—just across the river from Trastevere—is still home to Rome's Jewish community and retains fragments of its Jewish heritage.

The synagogue (rebuilt in 1904) stands at the heart of the former seven-acre ghetto. Inside, take in the impressive square dome, painted with the colors of the rainbow. An accompanying museum shows off Jewish artifacts from ancient to modern times.

Behind the synagogue is a square called Largo 16 Ottobre 1943, named for the day when Nazi trucks parked here to take Jews to concentration camps. Eventually 2,000 Jews were carried off, only a few returned, and the ghetto never recovered.

The big ancient gateway is the Portico d'Ottavia, which has ruins that were incorporated into a medieval church. This Christian church sat in the middle of the ghetto, where Jews were forced to sit through Saturday sermons.

Via del Portico d'Ottavia is the main drag of today's small Jewish community. Notice a few kosher restaurants, shops selling Judaica and Jewish-themed art, posters for community events, men wearing yarmulkes, political graffiti, a Jewish school (the big yellow building), and security measures to prevent terrorism. In the pedestrianized square, the older folks gather to gossip and kvetch.

Finish at the traditional Jewish bakery with some braided challah bread, almond macaroons, or a little fruitcake dubbed a "Jewish pizza."

► *The synagogue and Jewish Museum (Museo Ebraico) are accessible to tourists only with a €11 guided tour. Open April-Sept Sun-Thu 10:00-18:00, Fri 10:00-16:00, shorter hours off-season, closed Sat year-round; last entry 45 minutes before closing. Modest dress is required. Located on Lungotevere dei Cenci, tel. 06-6840-0661, www.museoebraico. roma.it.*

You can ⌒ download a free Rick Steves audio tour of the Jewish Ghetto (✪ see page 195).

Sights *(margin)*

SOUTH ROME

These second-tier but interesting sights are strung along Metro line B, south of the city.

In South Rome you'll find ancient ruins, including the famous Appian Way with its underground catacombs. There's the gritty-but-trendy neighborhood of Testaccio. South of that is a major pilgrimage church, and farther still is the eerie suburb-of-the-future built by Mussolini, called E.U.R.

To find these sights, ✪ see the foldout color map.

▲Appian Way and Catacombs

The famous ancient Roman road offers three attractions: the old road itself, lined with crumbling tombs and monuments; the underground Christian catacombs; and the peaceful atmosphere of pine and cypress trees. Concentrate on the sight-packed stretch of road between the Tomb of Cecilia Metella and the Domine Quo Vadis Church.

The Appian Way once ran 430 miles from Rome to the Adriatic port of Brindisi, the gateway to Greece. After Spartacus' slave revolt was suppressed (71 B.C.), the road was lined with 6,000 crucified slaves as a warning. Today you can walk (or bike) some stretches of the road, rattling over original paving stones and past mile markers. The two most impressive pagan sights are the ruins of the Tomb of Cecilia Metella (a massive cylindrical burial place for a rich noble woman) and the Circus of Maxentius (a once-grand chariot race track).

When the Christian faith permeated Rome, Christians were buried along the Appian Way in labyrinthine underground tunnels called catacombs. Legends say that early Christians actually lived in the catacombs to escape persecution, but that's not true.

The two major catacombs—**San Sebastiano** and **San Callisto**—are a few hundred yards apart. At either place, a guide leads you underground to see burial niches (but no bones), faded frescoes, memorial chapels to saints, Christian symbols (doves, fish, anchors), and graffiti by early Christian tag artists. Both catacombs are quite similar, so pick one to tour.

The tiny Domine Quo Vadis Church marks the spot where Peter, fleeing Rome, saw a vision of Christ. Peter asked Jesus, "Lord, where are you going?" (*"Domine quo vadis?"* in Latin), to which Christ replied, "I am going to Rome to be crucified again." The vision shamed Peter into returning to the wicked city.

▸ *Most Appian Way sights are open Tuesday through Sunday, closed Monday. However...*

The Catacombs of San Callisto (€8) are open Thu-Tue 9:00-12:00 & 14:00-17:00, closed Wed and Late Jan-late Feb. 30 minute tours depart about every half-hour. Located at Via Appia Antica 110, tel. 06-5130-1580 or 06-513-0151, www.catacombe.roma.it.

The Catacombs of San Sebastiano (€8) are open Mon-Sat 10:00-17:00,

Appian Way, site of the catacombs

Testaccio's ancient pyramid and city gate

closed Sun and late Nov-late Dec. Located at Via Appia Antica 136, tel. 06-785-0350, www.catacombe.org.

To get there and back, I recommend this route: Take a taxi (€20) or bus (#660 from the Colli Albani Metro stop) to the Tomb of Cecilia Metella. Walk the Appian Way to the Catacombs of San Sebastiano. From there, avoid the most-trafficked stretch of road by taking the peaceful pedestrian path (enter through the arch at #126) which leads to the Catacombs of San Callisto and continues to the Domine Quo Vadis Church. From there, catch bus #118 to the Piramide Metro stop. You're back in central Rome—"Quo vadis," pilgrim?

Baths of Caracalla (Terme di Caracalla)

Inaugurated by Emperor Caracalla in A.D. 216, this massive bath complex could accommodate 1,600 visitors at a time. Today it's just a shell—a huge shell—with all of its sculptures and most of its mosaics moved to museums. You'll see a two-story roofless brick building surrounded by a garden, bordered by ruined walls. Two large exercise rooms flank the former swimming pool.

The baths functioned until Goths severed the aqueducts in the sixth century. In modern times, grand operas are performed here during the summer (see www.operaroma.it).

▶ *€6. Open Tue-Sun 9:00 until one hour before sunset (19:00 in summer, 16:30 in winter), and Mon 9:00-14:00, Tue-Sun 9:00 until one hour before sunset: April-Aug until 19:15, Sept until 19:00, Oct until 18:30, off-season closes as early as 16:30; last entry one hour before closing. From the Circus Maximus Metro stop, walk five minutes south along Via delle Terme di Caracalla, or take bus #714 from Termini Station. Tel. 06-3996-7700, www.archeoroma.beniculturali.it.*

Testaccio Neighborhood

You can spend a pleasant hour exploring several fascinating but lesser sights near the Piramide Metro stop, in the creative, postindustrial neighborhood of Testaccio. Working-class since ancient times, Testaccio has recently gone trendy-bohemian. Visitors wander through an awkward mix of yuppie and proletarian worlds. Even if you don't see it, you'll perhaps sense the "Keep Testaccio for the Testaccians" graffiti.

The covered **Mercato di Testaccio** dominates the center of the neighborhood. This is hands-down the best, most authentic food market

in Rome (Mon-Sat until 14:00). It's where Romans shop while tourists flock to Campo de' Fiori.

Monte Testaccio, a small hill, is actually a 115-foot-tall ancient trash pile made of broken *testae*—broken pots. Two thousand years ago, old pottery jars were discarded here, and slowly, Rome's lowly eighth hill was built. Today, the hill is surrounded by a mix of gritty car-repair places and trendy bars. For the full experience, be here after 21:00, when the youthful nightlife kicks in.

The **Pyramid of Gaius Cestius** stands next to the Piramide Metro stop. This 90-foot-tall marble-over-brick structure was built around 30 B.C., at a time when Mark Antony was wooing Cleopatra, and exotic Egyptian styles were in vogue.

Nearby is the **Porta San Paolo,** a gate in the 12-mile Aurelian Wall (third century) that once encircled the city. Inside the gate is a tiny (free) museum, the Museo della Via Ostiense, displaying models of Ostia Antica, Rome's ancient port (open Tue-Sun 9:00-13:00, closed Mon).

The **Protestant Cemetery** is a peaceful, tomb-filled park. Upon entering, head 90 degrees left to find the tomb of English poet John Keats (1795-1821), in the far corner. The tomb of fellow poet Percy Shelley

(1792-1822) is straight ahead from the entrance, up the hill, at the base of the stubby tower. Both Romantic poets came on the Grand Tour and—"captivated by the fatal charms of Rome," as Shelley wrote—never left (€3 donation. Mon-Sat 9:00-17:00, Sun until 13:00, www.cemetery rome.it).

Sights Farther South

These three sights outside the city center are easily reached by Metro.

▲**Montemartini Museum:** This never-crowded, kid-friendly place has a dreamy collection of 400 ancient statues set evocatively in a classic 1932 electric power plant.

▸ *€7.50. Open Tue-Sun 9:00-19:00, closed Mon. Located at Via Ostiense 106, Metro: Garbatella. Tel 06-0608, www.centralemontemartini.org.*

▲**St. Paul's Outside the Walls:** This was the last major construction project of Imperial Rome (A.D. 380) and the largest church in Christendom until St. Peter's. The interior, lit by alabaster windows, is vast—if a bit sterile. What is believed to be the sarcophagus of St. Paul is visible under the altar.

▸ *Free. Open daily 7:00-18:30. Modest dress code enforced. Located a short walk from Metro: Basilica San Paolo, www.basilicasanpaolo.org.*

E.U.R.: This is the 1930s-era planned city built by Italy's dictator, Benito Mussolini, to show off the wonders of his fascist society. E.U.R.'s key landmark is the lone skyscraper understandably nicknamed the "Square Colosseum." Today, E.U.R. (pronounced AY-oor) is worth a trip for its Museum of Roman Civilization (may be closed for renovation), its Italian modernism (for architecture buffs), and to see what our world might look like if Hitler and Mussolini had won the war.

E.U.R.'s "Square Colosseum"

Ostia Antica—Pompeii without the crowds

▶ *To reach E.U.R., get off at Metro stop Magliana for the "Square Colosseum," or Metro stop Fermi for the Museum of Roman Civilization.*

NEAR ROME

An hour or two ride by bus or train can get you out of the big-city bustle to some peaceful sights. Think of these as day trips, as they'll consume most of a sightseeing day.

▲▲Ostia Antica

The ancient Roman port city of Ostia is similar to the famous ruins of Pompeii but a lot closer and less touristed. Wandering around, you'll see ruined warehouses, apartment flats, mansions, shopping arcades, and baths that served a once-thriving port of 60,000 people.

Located at the mouth *(ostium)* of the Tiber, Ostia was Rome's gateway to the open seas. At the peak of the Empire, it was a Europe-wide commercial shipping hub, handling the big business of keeping more than a million Romans fed and in sandals.

Enter through the main city gate (Porta Romana) and walk down the long, straight main drag (Decumanus Maximus), past once-vast warehouses. Pop into the well-preserved Theater, which could seat 4,000 and is still used today. Behind the stage, explore the Square of the Guilds, once lined with more than 60 offices. The sidewalks have mosaics advertising their lines of business—grain silos, an elephant for ivory traders, boats for ship-makers, and the symbol of Ostia itself, a lighthouse.

Continuing down main street, detour right down Via dei Molini, and find the Mill (Molino), the tavern (Insula of the Thermopolium), and a typical apartment house (the Insula of the Paintings). Ostia's working class lived in cramped, noisy multistory buildings, with no plumbing, heat, or kitchens—they survived on take-out food.

The main street spills into the town's main square, or Forum, dominated by the Capitolium temple, dedicated to the trinity of Jupiter, Juno, and Minerva. Now just a brick core, the temple was originally huge, fronted with columns and faced with gleaming white marble.

Near the Forum Baths (Terme del Foro), find the latrine. Yes, those 20 holes are toilets, each with a cutout to hold the sponge-on-a-stick used instead of toilet paper. Rushing water below the seats did the flushing. Privacy? Even today there's no Italian word for it.

Finish your sightseeing with the fine statue museum, then visit the cafeteria and pop something tasty into your *ostium maximus*.

▶ *€8, €11 during special exhibits. Open April-Aug Tue-Sun 8:30-19:15, progressively shorter hours off-season, closed Mon year-round, last entry one hour before closing. Tel. 06-5635-0215, www.ostiaantica. beniculturali.it. A free ∩ Rick Steves audio tour of the site is available (☺ see page 195).*

Getting There: From Rome's Piramide Metro stop (also a train station), catch any train headed toward Lido—they all stop at Ostia Antica along the way. A single €1.50 Metro ticket covers the one-way train ride. Arriving at Ostia Antica, leave the train station, cross over the blue skybridge, and walk straight down Via della Stazione di Ostia Antica until you reach the parking lot and entrance.

▲Tivoli: The Villa d'Este and Hadrian's Villa

At the edge of the Sabine Hills, 18 miles east of Rome, sits the pleasant medieval hill town of Tivoli. Today, it's famous for two very different villas, or country estates: the Villa d'Este (a 16th-century mansion with playful fountains in the gardens) and Hadrian's Villa (the Roman emperor's large complex of buildings, now in ruins).

The Villa d'Este: Cardinal Ippolito d'Este, a sophisticated lover of luxury, leveled a monastery at Tivoli and replaced it with his personal pleasure palace (1550s). It's a watery wonderland—a mansion with terraced gardens and fountains on a cool hill with breath-catching views. Its design and statuary were inspired by (and looted from) the ancient villa of Hadrian.

The Villa d'Este's star attraction is hundreds of Baroque fountains, most of which are still gravity-powered. The Aniene River, frazzled into countless threads, weaves its way entertainingly through the villa. At the bottom of the garden, the exhausted little streams once again team up to make a sizable river.

Hike through the gardens, and then enjoy the terrace restaurant on the highest level of the garden, opportunely placed to catch cool afternoon sea breezes as you gaze across the plain of Rome.

Hadrian's Villa: Emperor Hadrian (ruled A.D. 117-138) built this country residence as an escape from the heat of Rome and the pressures of court life. Hadrian ruled at the peak of the Roman Empire, when it stretched from England to the Euphrates and encompassed countless diverse cultures. The Spanish-born Hadrian—an architect, lover of Greek culture, and great traveler—had personally visited many of the lands he ruled. At Tivoli, he created a microcosm of his empire, re-creating famous structures from around the world—an Egyptian-style canal, a Greek-style stoa, and so on. The Teatro Marittimo is a circular palace set on an artificial island. Here Hadrian could sit, at the symbolic center of his vast empire, and ponder what might become of it.

▶ *Villa d'Este: €8, €11 with special exhibits. Open daily May-Aug 9:00-19:30, April and Sept until 19:00, closes earlier off-season, last entry 1.5 hours before closing. Tel. 0774-382-733, www.villadestetivoli.info.*

Hadrian's Villa (Villa Adriana): €8, €11 with special exhibits, cash only. Open April-Sept daily 9:00-19:00, closes as early as 17:00 off-season, last entry 1.5 hours before closing. Tel. 0774-382-733.

Getting to Tivoli: From Rome's Metro stop Ponte Mammolo, take the local blue Cotral bus to Tivoli (45 minutes, 3/hour). The Villa d'Este is in the center of town near the Tivoli bus stop. To continue to Hadrian's Villa (2.5 miles outside Tivoli), catch orange "CAT" city bus #4 or #4X.

Hadrian's Villa, outside Rome, was where the emperor retreated to ponder his vast empire.

Sleeping

Choosing the right neighborhood is as important as choosing the right hotel. All of my recommended accommodations are in safe, pleasant neighborhoods convenient to sightseeing: The **Termini Train Station** neighborhood is handy for public transit and services, though not particularly charming. Hotels near **Ancient Rome** are close to the Colosseum and Roman Forum. The most romantic ambience is in neighborhoods near the **Pantheon** and **Campo de' Fiori.** Equally pleasant, if a bit rougher, is **Trastevere.** Finally, hotels near **Vatican City** put St. Peter's and the Vatican Museums at your doorstep.

I like hotels that are clean, central, friendly, quiet, good-value, and small enough to have a hands-on owner and stable staff. Four of these six virtues means it's a keeper.

A Typical Rome Hotel Room

Double rooms listed in this book average around €150 (including a private bathroom). They range from a low of roughly €85 to €350-plus (spacious, elegant places with all the modern conveniences).

A typical €150 double room in Rome will have one double bed or two twins. There's a bathroom in the room with a toilet, sink, and shower. The room has a telephone, a TV, and often a small fridge with drinks for sale. At this price, the room probably has air-conditioning (a must in summer). It will be upstairs from street level, but there's likely a (small) elevator. Single rooms, triples, and quads will have similar features.

Breakfast is usually included in the price. It's a self-service buffet of (at its most generous) cereal, ham, cheese, yogurt, and juice, while a waitress takes your coffee order.

The hotel will have Internet access, either Wi-Fi or a public terminal in the lobby. At many of my listings, at least one of these options is free. The staff speaks at least enough English to get by. Night clerks aren't paid enough to care deeply about problems that may arise.

Making Reservations

Reserve several weeks or even months in advance in peak season (mid-March-mid-July and Sept-Oct) or for a major holiday. Do it by phone, through the hotel's website, or with an email that reads something like this:

Dear Hotel Italia,

I would like to reserve a double room for 2 people for 3 nights, arriving 19 July and departing 22 July. If possible, I would like a quiet room with a double bed (not twin beds), air-conditioning, and a bathroom inside the room. Please let me know if a room is available and the price. Thank you.

If they require your credit-card number for a deposit, you can send it by email (I do), but it's safer via phone, the hotel's secure website, or split between two emails. Once your room is booked, print out the confirmation, and reconfirm your reservation with a phone call or email a day or two in advance (alert them if you'll be arriving after 17:00). If canceling a reservation, some hotels require advance notice—otherwise they may bill you. Even if there's no penalty, it's polite to give at least three days' notice.

Hotel Price Code

$$$$	**Splurge:** Most rooms over €170
$$$	**Pricier:** €130-170
$$	**Moderate:** €90-130
$	**Budget:** €50-90
¢	**Hostel/Backpacker:** Under €50
RS%	**Rick Steves discount**

These rates are for a standard double room with breakfast during high season; they don't include a €3-6/person room tax. For the best prices, book direct.

Budget Tips

To get the best rates, book directly with the hotel, not through a hotel-booking engine. Start with the hotel's website, looking for promo deals (official rates can drop 30 percent, especially at pricier hotels). Check rates every few days, as prices can change daily depending on demand. Email several hotels to ask for their best price and compare offers—you may be astonished at the range. When you contact the hotel, you may get a cheaper rate if you offer to pay cash, stay at least three nights, or simply ask for a cheaper room. Some of my listed hotels offer a "Rick Steves discount" for readers of this book—it's worth asking when you reserve your room. Off-season (Nov-mid-March and mid-July-Aug), fearless negotiators can arrive without a reservation late on a slow day and start talking.

Besides hotels, there are cheaper alternatives. Bed-and-breakfasts (B&Bs) offer a personal touch at a fair price—www.bedandbreakfast.com and www.wheninromebandb.com are good resources. Airbnb.com makes it reasonably easy to find a place to sleep in someone's home. At nun-run convents, the beds are twins and English is often in short supply, but the price is right (reserve early)—check www.santasusanna.org (select "Coming to Rome"). All-ages hostels offer dorm beds (and a few doubles) for around €20-30 (sheets included) and come with curfews; try www.hostelworld.com.

Renting an apartment can save money if you're traveling as a family, staying more than a week, and planning to cook your own meals. Try www.vrbo.com, www.homeaway.com, or www.wantedinrome.com.

NEAR TERMINI TRAIN STATION: Via Firenze—A safe, quiet street near Piazza Repubblica (Metro), Via Nazionale (bus #40 and #64), and the train station (a 10-minute walk)

$$$$ Residenza Cellini Via Modena 5 tel. 06-4782-5204, www.residenzacellini.it	Slice of Neoclassical elegance, four-star service, breezy breakfast terrace, RS%
$$$$ Hotel Modigliani Via della Purificazione 42 tel. 06-4281-5226, www.hotelmodigliani.com	Bright, minimalist, in-love-with-life style, generous lounge, garden, energetic staff, RS%
$$$$ IQ Hotel Via Firenze 8 tel. 06-488-0465, www.iqhotelroma.it	Modern building with fresh and spacious rooms, rooftop garden and play area
$$$ Hotel Oceania Via Firenze 38 tel. 06-482-4696, www.hoteloceania.it	Peaceful, spacious manor house w/terrace, Stefano continues family tradition of thoughtful service, RS%
$$$ Hotel Aberdeen Via Firenze 48 tel. 06-482-3920, www.hotelaberdeen.it	Modern quality plus friendliness from Annamaria and sisters, RS%
$$ Hotel Nardizzi Americana Via Firenze 38 tel. 06-488-0035, www.hotelnardizzi.it	Pleasant rooms and rooftop terrace, excellent value, RS%
$$ Hotel Margaret Via Antonio Salandra 6 tel. 06-482-4285, www.hotelmargaret.net	Welcoming rooms with modern basics and Impressionist prints, RS%

NEAR TERMINI: Between Via Nazionale and Santa Maria Maggiore—close to Termini Metro

$$$ Hotel Opera Roma Via Firenze 11 tel. 06-487-1787, www.hoteloperaroma.com	Contemporary furnishings and marble accents in spacious but dark rooms, RS%
$$$ Hotel Sonya Via del Viminale 58 tel. 06-481-9911, www.hotelsonya.it	Well-equipped, high-tech rooms, Farhad bakes daily for above-average breakfast, RS%
$$$ Hotel Selene Roma Via del Viminale 8 tel. 06-474-4781, www.hoteleleneroma.it	Spread over several floors, elegant furnishings and room to breathe, RS%

$$ Hotel Montreal Via Carlo Alberto 4 tel. 06-445-7797, www.hotelmontrealroma.com	Bright, secure business-class place in so-so surroundings, run with care, RS%
$$ Hotel Italia Roma Via Venezia 18 tel. 06-482-8355, www.hotelitaliaroma.it	Bright rooms, quiet street, busy locale, thoughtful staff, decent annex rooms, too, RS%
$$ Gulliver's Lodge Via Cavour 101 tel. 06-9727-3787, www.gulliverslodge.com	Busy neighborhood but secure and quiet, no lobby, in-room DVDs, RS%
$ Suore di Santa Elisabetta Via dell'Olmata 9 tel. 06-488-8271, www.csse-roma.com	Tranquil convent, tidy twin-bed rooms, 23:00 curfew, book early for super value
SLEEPING CHEAPLY, NORTHEAST OF TERMINI TRAIN STATION: Zero ambience, but safe and a good value	
¢ The Beehive Via Marghera 8 tel. 06-4470-4553, www.the-beehive.com	Homey American-run all-ages hostel, artsy-mod double rooms and eight-bed dorms
$ Hotel Select Garden Via V. Bachelet 6 tel. 06-445-6383, www.hotelselectgarden.com	Modern, quiet, welcoming refuge run by cheery family, modern art, lemony garden, RS%
$ Hotel Sileo Via Magenta 39 tel. 06-445-0246, www.hotelsileo.com	Shiny chandeliers in dim rooms, friendly owners speak limited English, air-con, RS%
¢ Funny Palace Hostel Via Varese 33 tel. 06-4470-3523, www.hostelfunny.com	Quiet four-person dorms and stark-but-clean doubles, launderette next door
¢ Yellow Hostel Via Palestro 44 tel. 06-4938-2682, www.yellowhostel.com	Dorms for ages 18-45 only, some all-ages private rooms, hip yet sane, no curfew

Sleeping

NEAR ANCIENT ROME: Between the Colosseum (Metro: Colosseo or Cavour) and Piazza Venezia (major bus hub)	
$$$$ Hotel Lancelot Via Capo d'Africa 47 tel. 06-7045-0615, www.lancelothotel.com	Elegant, quiet refuge with B&B ambience, shady courtyard, restaurant, bar, view terrace, RS%
$$$ Nicolas Inn B&B Via Cavour 295 tel. 328-555-3004, www.nicolasinn.com	Delightful, spacious and bright, run by friendly Francois and American Melissa, RS%
$$ Hotel Paba Via Cavour 266 tel. 06-4782-4902, www.hotelpaba.com, email to reserve: info@hotelpaba.com	Cozy, chocolate-box-tidy rooms, overlooks busy Via Cavour but quiet enough, RS%
$ Hotel Rosetta Via Cavour 295 tel. 06-4782-3069, www.rosettahotel.com	Homey, family-run pensione, minimal (no lounge or breakfast) but good location
$$$$ Nerva Boutique Hotel Via Tor de' Conti 3 tel. 06-678-1835, www.hotelnerva.com	Three-star slice of tranquility by Roman Forum, overpriced but rates are soft, RS%
$$ Casa Il Rosario Via Sant'Agata dei Goti 10 tel. 06-679-2346, irodopre@tin.it	Peaceful convent, twin-bed simplicity, good neighborhood, 23:00 curfew, some rooms with air-con, book early
NEAR CAMPO DE' FIORI: Winding lanes, fountains, markets, restaurants—maximum Roman ambience	
$$$$ Casa di Santa Brigida Via di Monserrato 54 tel. 06-6889-2596, www.brigidine.org	Lavish convent overlooking elegant Piazza Farnese, twin beds only but a worthwhile splurge
$$$ Hotel Smeraldo Via dei Chiavari 20 tel. 06-687-5929, www.smeraldoroma.com	Impersonal staff, clean, air-con, flowery roof terrace, similar annex, great deal, RS%
$$ Hotel Arenula Via Santa Maria de' Calderari 47 tel. 06-687-9454, www.hotelarenula.com	Southeast of Campo de' Fiori in Jewish Ghetto, good value but gym-like ambience, RS%

CLOSE TO THE PANTHEON: Lively day and night, many sights and restaurants	
$$$$ Hotel Nazionale Piazza Montecitorio 131 tel. 06-695-001, www.hotelnazionale.it	Big, stuffy four-star hotel, lush public spaces, uniformed staff, worthy splurge
$$$ Albergo Santa Chiara Via di Santa Chiara 21 tel. 06-687-2979, www.albergosantachiara.com	Big and professional, fine staff, marbled elegance, quiet and spacious rooms, RS%
$$$$ Hotel Due Torri Vicolo del Leonetto 23 tel. 06-6880-6956, www.hotelduetorriroma.com	Professional and accommodating, big lounge, small rooms, overpriced but great quiet location
IN TRASTEVERE: Less central and a bit rough around the edges, but typically Roman	
$$$$ Hotel Santa Maria Vicolo del Piede 2 tel. 06-589-4626, www.hotelsantamaria.info, email to reserve: info@hotelsantamaria.info	Lazy hacienda amid romantic medieval skyline, small well-equipped rooms, orange-tree patio, RS%
$$$$ Residenza Arco dei Tolomei Via dell'Arco de' Tolomei 27 tel. 06-5832-0819, www.bbarcodeitolomei.com	Small, unique, antique-filled rooms in quiet aristocratic setting, book early
$$$$ Hotel San Francesco Via Jacopa de' Settesoli 7 tel. 06-5830-0051, www.hotelsanfrancesco.net, email to reserve: hotelsanfrancesco@gmail.com	Big yet welcoming, inviting roof terrace, sits at the far end of the Trastevere action
$$$ Arco del Lauro B&B Via dell'Arco de' Tolomei 29 tel. 06-9784-0350, www.arcodellauro.it	Whitewashed, straightforward rooms in good location, friendly welcome, 4-night minimum for peak weekends

NEAR VATICAN CITY: Workaday neighborhood handy to Metro and major sights

$$$$ Hotel Alimandi Vaticano Viale Vaticano 99 tel. 06-3974-5562, www.alimandivaticanohotel.com	Facing the Vatican Museums, spacious rooms with all the modern conveniences
$$ Hotel Museum Via Tunisi 8 tel. 06-3972-3941, www.hotelmuseum.it	Good value, friendly Alimandi family, modern perfumed rooms, fun public areas
$$$ Hotel Gerber Via degli Scipioni 241 tel. 06-321-6485, www.hotelgerber.it	Family-run with well-polished, business-like air-con rooms in quiet residential area, RS%
$$ Casa Valdese Via Alessandro Farnese 18 tel. 06-321-5362, www.casavaldeseroma.it	Big, quiet rooms, efficient but institutional, breezy communal rooftop with views, RS%
$$ Casa per Ferie S.M. alle Fornaci Piazza Santa Maria alle Fornaci 27 tel. 06-3936-7632, www.trinitaridematha.it	Convent-esque but user-friendly, starkly utilitarian twin-bedded rooms, book early

Eating

The Italians are masters of the art of fine eating. Lingering over a multi-course meal at an outdoor table watching a parade of passersby while you sip wine with loved ones...it's one of Rome's great pleasures.

I list a full range of eateries, from budget options for a quick bite to multicourse splurges with maximum ambience. They're located in neighborhoods handy to sightseeing, hotels, and atmosphere—✪ see the maps on pages 179-182. Many of my listings offer outdoor seating, even in winter, thanks to patio heaters. I prefer mom-and-pop, personality-driven places, with a local clientele. I appreciate both quality food and atmosphere, and my listings offer a reasonable balance of both.

Restaurant Price Code

$$$$ Splurge: Most main courses over €20
 $$$ Pricier: €15-20
  $$ Moderate: €10-15
   $ Budget: Under €10

Based on the average cost of a typical main course (pasta or *secondi*).
Pizza by the slice and takeaway is $; a basic trattoria or sit-down pizzeria is $$; a casual but more upscale restaurant is $$$; and a swanky splurge is $$$$.

When in Rome…

When in Rome, I eat on the Roman schedule. For breakfast, I eat at the hotel or grab a pastry and cappuccino at the neighborhood bar. Lunch—which traditionally was the biggest Italian meal of the day—is now more commonly a quick pasta or a take-out sandwich (panino or *tramezzino*), great for an atmospheric picnic. In the late afternoon, many Romans enjoy an after-work aperitivo and snack *(spuntino)*. Dinner is the time for slowing down and savoring a restaurant meal.

Restaurants

Restaurants serve lunch 13:00-15:00 (and rarely open their doors before noon). Dinner is served to Romans from 20:00-22:00 and to tourists at 19:00 (quality restaurants rarely open any earlier).

While the word *ristorante* is self-explanatory, you'll also see other names for sit-down Italian restaurants. *Trattoria* and *osteria* imply a more homey establishment, and *pizzerias, enotecas,* and *birrerias* specialize more in pizza, wine, and beer than full-course meals, but there are no hard-and-fast distinctions.

A full restaurant meal comes in courses: an antipasto, a plate of pasta, salad (either before or after the pasta course—your choice), the meat course, dessert, coffee, liqueurs, and so on. It can take hours, and the costs can add up quickly, so plan your strategy before sitting down to a restaurant meal.

For light eaters, there's nothing wrong with ordering a single dish as

your meal—a plate of pasta, a pizza, an antipasto, or a salad. A good strategy for light-eating couples is to share a total of four dishes—e.g., one antipasto, one pasta, one meat course, and one dessert (or whatever combination appeals). Larger groups can share a variety of dishes from several courses, family style. Another good-value option common in Rome is self-serve buffets of cold and cooked *antipasti* (like a salad bar).

If you want a full meal at a predictable price, consider the *menu turistico*—a fixed-price multicourse meal where you can choose from a list of menu items. It includes the service charge, and is usually a good value for non-gourmets.

In Rome, only rude waiters rush you. For speedier service, be prepared with your next request whenever a waiter happens to grace your table. You'll have to ask for the bill—mime-scribble on your raised palm or ask: *"Il conto?"*

Quick Budget Meals

Rome offers many budget options for hungry travelers.

Italian "bars" are not taverns but cafés. These neighborhood hangouts serve coffee, sandwiches (grilled *panini* or cold *tramezzini*), mini-pizzas, pre-made salads, fresh squeezed orange juice *(spremuta),* and drinks from the cooler.

Various cafeteria-style places (*tavola calda, rosticceria,* or just "cafeteria") dish out fast and cheap cooked meals to eat there or take out. You can buy pizza by the slice at little hole-in-the-wall places, sold by weight (100 grams for a small slice). A wine bar *(enoteca)* sells wine by the glass, but they also serve meat-and-cheese-type plates for the business crowd at lunch and happy hour. Trendy cocktail lounges offer free happy-hour buffets for the price of an (overpriced) drink—often a good value.

At any eating establishment (however humble), be aware that the price of your food and drink may be 20-40 percent more if you consume it while sitting at a table instead of standing at the bar. This two-tier price system will always be clearly posted. Also, at many bars, the custom is to first pay the cashier for what you want, then hand the receipt to a barista who serves you.

Picnicking saves euros and time, lets you sample regional specialties, and puts you in contact with everyday Romans in the marketplace. Buy a sandwich or slice of pizza "to go" *(da portar via),* get fruit at the corner grocery store, a bottle of wine, refill your water bottle at a public tap...and dine like an emperor amid atmospheric surroundings. Note that Rome discourages people from picnicking at historic monuments, but it's rarely enforced for discreet adults. Also, when buying produce, it's customary to let the merchant pick it out. If something is a mystery, ask for a small taste—*"un assaggio, per favore."*

Roman Cuisine

Rome has a few specialties: *spaghetti alla carbonara* (in egg-bacon sauce), *gnocchi alla romana* (dumplings), *carciofi alla giudia* (artichokes), *saltimbocca alla romana* (veal), pecorino romano cheese (from ewe's milk), and *trippa alla romana* (tripe—intestines—as good as it sounds).

No meal in Italy is complete without wine. Even the basic house wine (*vino da tavola* or *vino della casa*) is a good choice. The region around Rome produces Frascati (an inexpensive dry white) or Torre Ercolana (an expensive, aged, dense red). You'll also find lots of Chiantis and Montepulcianos from Tuscany (for an upgrade, pay more for a Brunello di Montalcino); well-aged Barbaresco and Barolo from Piedmont; and crisp white Orvieto Classico.

Popular before-dinner *aperitvos* are Campari and Cynar. After-dinner liqueurs include *amaro* (various brands) and anise-flavored Sambuca.

Italian coffee is excellent. Even basic bars serve espresso, *macchiatos,* and cappuccinos. In the summer, Romans like a sugared iced coffee called *caffè freddo.* Streetside vendors sell *grattachecca* (grah-tah-KEK-kah): shaved ice with fruit syrup.

For dessert, try *Tartufo*—a rich dark-chocolate gelato ball. Or pick up a cup or cone of gelato at a *gelateria,* and join the rest of Rome, strolling the streets and enjoying a slice of edible art.

For Foodies: For food-themed guided walks through Rome's colorful marketplace neighborhoods, see eatingitalyfoodtours.com. For evening wine-tasting classes, see vinoroma.com.

NEAR PIAZZA NAVONA (see map on page 179)

1	**$$ Pizzeria da Baffetto** Via del Governo Vecchio 114 tel. 06-686-1617	Rustic, energetic local favorite west of piazza, jammed after 20:00; cash only (daily 12:00-15:30 & 18:30 until late)
2	**$$ Ristorante del Fico** Via della Pace 34 tel. 06-688-91373)	Sprawling, rustic-chic place that feels like a huge Italian saloon (nightly from 19:30)
3	**$$ Cul de Sac** On Piazza Pasquino tel. 06-6880-1094	Skinny trattoria packed with wine-loving locals, try salumi sampler or full meal (daily 12:00-24:00)
4	**$ L'Insalata Ricca** Largo dei Chiavari 85 tel. 06-6880-3656 Piazza Pasquino 72 tel. 06-6830-7881	Popular chain specializing in €10-12 salads, pastas, and meal deals, two locations (daily 12:00-24:00)
5	**$$ Ristorante Pizzeria "da Francesco"** Piazza del Fico 29 tel. 06-686-4009	Bustling, unpretentious with hardworking young staff, great seating inside and out (daily 12:00-15:30 & 19:00-24:00)

CLOSE TO THE PANTHEON (see map on page 179)

6	**$$$$ Ristorante da Fortunato** Via del Pantheon 55 tel. 06-679-2788 www.ristorantefortunato.it	Surprisingly reasonable dress-up classics (figure €50/person); people-watching outside; elegant seating inside; reservations smart (daily 12:30-23:30)
7	**$$ Enoteca Corsi** Via del Gesù 87 tel. 06-679-0821	Friendly wine shop serves lunch only; straightforward traditional cuisine at great prices (Mon-Sat 12:00-15:30, Thu-Fri also 19:00-22:30, closed Sun)
8	**$$ Miscellanea** Via della Palombella 34 tel. 06-6813-5318	Much-loved Mikki keeps foreign-study students well-fed with hearty sandwiches, salads, pasta (daily 9:00-24:00; may close in 2018)
9	**$$ Osteria da Mario** Piazza delle Coppelle 51 tel. 06-6880-6349	Mom-and-pop joint with traditional favorites (Mon-Sat 12:30-15:30 & 19:00-23:00)

⑩	**$$ Osteria delle Coppelle** Piazza delle Coppelle 54 tel. 06-4550-2826	Slapdash and trendy; traditional dishes and fun selection of €3 cicchetti—Italian-style tapas (daily 12:30-16:00 & 19:00 until late)
⑪	**$ Frullati Pascucci** Via di Torre Argentina 20 tel. 06-686-4816	Convenient for takeaways, fruit, and salads (Mon-Sat 6:00-23:00, closed Sun)
⑫	**Supermercato Coop** Via Giustiniani 18	Supermarket half a block west of the Pantheon, convenient for picnic supplies (daily 8:30-22:00)
⑬	**Gelateria Giolitti** Via Uffici del Vicario 40	Rome's most famous gelato in an Old World setting (long hours daily)
⑭	**Crèmeria Monteforte** Via della Rotonda 22 tel. 06-686-7720	Gelato, super-creamy cremolati sorbets (Tue-Sun 10:00-24:00)
⑮	**Gelateria San Crispino** Piazza della Maddalena 3	Gelato in small portions, natural ingredients (daily 12:00-24:00)
IN NORTH ROME: Near the Ara Pacis and Spanish Steps (see map on page 179)		
⑯	**$$$ Ristorante il Gabriello** Via Vittoria 51 tel. 06-6994-0810 www.ilgabriello.it	Small, inviting respite, trust waiter's suggestions or €45 "Claudio's Extravaganza"; slightly dressy; reservations smart (Mon-Sat 10:00 23:00)
⑰	**$$ Palatium** 5 blocks in front of the Spanish Steps Via Frattina 94 tel. 06-6920-2132	Crisp, modern eatery promoting local products; generous, shareable cheese-and-salumi plates; huge wine selection (daily 9:00-22:30; may close in 2018)
⑱	**$$ Antica Enoteca** Via della Croce 76b tel. 06-679-0896 www.anticaenotecaroma.com	Bustling, atmospheric old restaurant and jam-packed wine bar, daily specials, €14 antipasti (daily 12:00-24:00)
⑲	**$$ Trattoria dal Cavalier Gino** Vicolo Rosini 4 tel. 06-687-3434	Tucked-away haunt of VIPs since 1963 (Gino's still there); cash only, reservations essential (Mon-Sat 13:00-14:45 & 20:00-22:30)

NEAR VATICAN CITY (see map on page 180)

20	**$$ Hostaria dei Bastioni** Via Leone IV 29 tel. 06-3972-3034	Emilio serves honest food near Vatican Museums; street-side seating or quiet interior (Mon-Sat 12:00-15:00 & 18:00-23:00)
21	**$ Forno Feliziani** Via Candia 61	Pizza by the slice, cafeteria-style dishes to eat in or take out (closed Sun) tel. 06-3973-7362
22	**$ L'Insalata Ricca** Piazza Risorgimento 5 tel. 06-3973-0387	Popular chain specializes in healthy salads, plus pasta and *secondi* (daily 12:00-23:30)
23	**$ Duecento Gradi** Piazza Risorgimento 3 tel. 06-3975-4239	A good bet for fresh and creative €5-8 sandwiches (daily 10:30-24:00)
24	**$$ Tre Pupazzi** A block northeast of St. Peter's Square Via Tre Pupazzi 1 tel. 06-6880-3220	Cheap eatery on interesting pedestrian-only street, Borgo Pio (Mon-Sat 12:00-15:00 & 19:00-23:00)
25	**$ Vecchio Borgo** Borgo Pio 27a tel. 06-8117-3585	Cheap to-go eatery, pizza by weight (Mon-Sat 9:30-22:30)
26	**$ Mercato Trionfale** Three blocks north of the Vatican Museums on Via Tunisi	Great for picnic supplies and photo-safaris (Mon-Sat roughly 7:00-14:00, Tue and Fri some stalls until 19:00)
27	**Supermarket Carrefour Express** Via Sebastiano Veniero 16	Near Mercato, handy for picnic supplies (Daily 8:00-20:30)
28	**Gelateria Old Bridge** Viale dei Bastioni di Michelangelo 3 tel. 06-4559-9961	Hearty scoops of gelato for tourists and nuns (daily 9:00-late)

IN TRASTEVERE AND NEAR CAMPO DE' FIORI (see map on page 181)

29	**$$ Trattoria da Lucia** Vicolo del Mattonato 2 tel. 06-580-3601	Simple, traditional food, good price, quintessential family-run scene since before World War II; cash only (Tue-Sun 12:30-15:00 & 19:30-23:00, closed Mon and much of Aug)

Eating

30	**$$ Trattoria da Olindo** Via del Mattonato 8 tel. 06-581-8835	Extreme hominess, like you're part of family—so don't expect smiles; cash only (Mon-Sat dinner served 19:30-22:30)
31	**$$ Pizzeria Dar Poeta** Vicolo del Bologna 45 tel. 06-588-0516	Friendly alley joint cranks out stellar wood-fired pizza (daily 12:00-24:00)
32	**$$ Osteria Ponte Sisto** Via Ponte Sisto 80 tel. 06-588-3411	Touristy, old-school feel and traditional Roman and Neapolitan cuisine (March-Oct Thu-Tue 12:30-15:00 & 19:00-23:30, closed Wed)
33	**$$$ Osteria La Gensola** Piazza della Gensola 15 tel. 06-581-6312 www.osterialagensola.it	Seafood restaurant with a rustic yet sophisticated living room (daily 13:00-15:00 & 19:30-23:00)
34	**$$ Pizzeria "Ai Marmi"** Viale Trastevere 53 tel. 06-580-0919	Bright and noisy festival of assembly-line pizza, jammed after 20:00; cash only (Thu-Tue 18:30 until late)
35	**$$ Cantina Ripagrande** Via San Francesco a Ripa 73 tel. 06-4547-6237	Simple, uncrowded romantic charm; happy-hour drinks and small buffet (daily 18:00-20:30)
36	**$$$$ Taverna Trilussa** Via del Politeama 23 tel. 06-581-8918 www.tavernatrilussa.it	Highest quality local classic dishes without pretense, spacious dining hall or outdoor terrace; reservations smart (Mon-Sat from 19:30)
37	**$$ Enoteca L'Angolo Divino** Via dei Balestrari 12 tel. 06-686-4413	Inviting little wine bar; tiny tables, tiny menu, smart advice, good wines by the glass (daily 11:00-15:00 &17:00-24:00, no afternoon closure Sun-Mon)
38	**$$$ Salumeria e Vineria Roscioli** Via dei Giubbonari 21 tel. 06-687-5287 www.salumeriaroscioli.com	Elegant enoteca with fine cheeses, meats, local dishes, and top-end wines; reservations a must (Mon-Sat 12:30-16:00 & 19:00-24:00, closed Sun)
39	**$$ Filetti di Baccalà** Largo dei Librari 88 tel. 06-686-4018	Cheap, fluorescent-lit greasy spoon, regulars eat deep-fried salt cod; cash only (Mon-Sat 17:30-23:00)

40	**$$$ Trattoria der Pallaro** Largo del Pallaro 15 tel. 06-6880-1488	Fixed-price €25 meal, eccentric staff and forgettable food but fun experience; cash only (daily 12:00-16:00 & 19:00-24:00)
41	**$$ Open Baladin Pub** Via degli Specchi 5 tel. 06-683-8989	Modern brewpub with Italian craft beers on tap, burgers, salads, and freshly made potato chips (daily 12:00-very late)
42	**$$ Sora Margherita** Piazza delle Cinque Scole 30 tel. 06-687-4216	Behind red curtain in Jewish ghetto, basic old-time Roman and Jewish dishes (reservations smart, lunch 12:30-15:00, dinner at 20:00 and 21:30, closed Sun and late Aug)

NEAR THE TREVI FOUNTAIN (see map on page 182)

43	**$ L'Antica Birreria Peroni** Via di San Marcello 19 tel. 06-679-5310	Rome's answer to a German beer hall: hearty mugs, fun food, giddy locals (Mon-Sat 12:00-24:00)
44	**$$ Osteria Sacro e Profano** Via dei Maroniti 29 tel. 06-679-1836	Spicy southern Italian food in old church, €15 antipasti sampler, satisfied tourists (Tue-Sun 12:00-15:00 & 18:00-23:00; may close in 2018)

IN ANCIENT ROME, NEAR THE COLOSSEUM (see map on page 182)

45	**$$ Enoteca Cavour 313** Via Cavour 313 tel. 06-678-5496	Wine bar with quality food, friendly service, mellow ambience for convenient lunch near Forum (daily 12:30-14:45 & 18:30-24:00)
46	**$ Caffè dello Studente** Via delle Terme di Tito 95 mobile 320-854-0333	Student crowds, decent toasted sandwiches, salads, pizzas (daily 7:30-20:00, closed Sun Nov-March)
47	**$$ Hostaria da Nerone** Via delle Terme di Tito 96 tel. 06-481-7952	Cozy place with homemade pasta, €10 choose-your-own antipasti plate makes quick lunch (Mon-Sat 12:00-15:00 & 19:00-23:00)
48	**$$ Terre e Domus** Foro Traiano 82 tel. 06-6994-0273	Modern little place; cool, peaceful, and well-lit; showcases local ingredients and provides jobs to out-of-work residents (daily 9:00-23:30)

Eating

NEAR TERMINI TRAIN STATION (see map on page 182)

49	**$$ Ristorante Da Giovanni** Via Antonio Salandra 1 tel. 06-485-950	Old-school, high-energy diner cranks out standard fare at great prices (Mon-Sat 12:00-15:00 & 19:00-22:00, closed Sun and Aug)
50	**$$$ Ristorante La Pentolaccia** Via Flavia 38 tel. 06-483-477 www.lapentolaccia.eu	Dressy, tourist-friendly place with tight seating, some romance, and classic Roman cooking (daily 12:00-15:00 & 17:30-23:00)
51	**$ Bufala e Pachino Pizza** Via Firenze 54 tel. 06-474-3668	Pizza by the slice and priced by weight— just point and tell them how much you'd like (daily 8:00-23:00)
52	**$$ Hostaria Romana** Via de Boccaccio 1 tel. 06-474-5284 www.hostariaromana.it	Busy, fun-loving bistro, fish and traditional, good €12 antipasti (Mon-Sat 12:30-15:00 & 19:15-23:00, closed Sun and Aug)
53	**$ Caffè Torino** Via Torino 40A tel. 06-474-2767	Good, fresh, hot dishes; peruse the enticing display, point at what you want, then wait to be served (Mon-Fri 6:00-17:00, closed Sat-Sun)
54	**$ Bar Firenze** Via Firenze 33 tel. 06-488-3862	Cafeteria-style quality lunch, inexpensive pastas, colorful sandwiches (daily 6:30-24:00)
55	**$$ Pizzeria Annicinquanta** Via Flavia 3 tel. 06-4201-0460	Neapolitan-style pizzas in a calm ambience (daily 12:30-15:30 & 19:30-24:00)
56	**$$ Target Restaurant** Via Torino 33 tel. 06-474-0066, www.targetrestaurant.it	Sleek and dressy, food that's reliably good, but pricey (daily 12:00-15:30 & 19:00-24:00)

Restaurants Close to the Pantheon & in North Rome

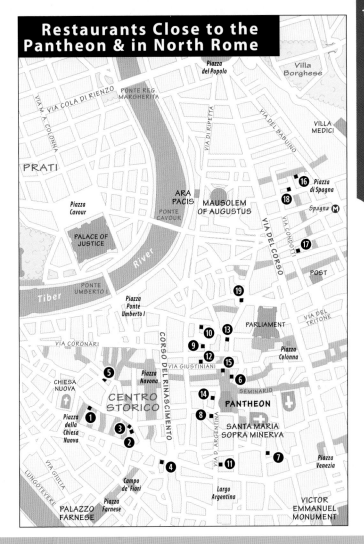

Restaurants Near Vatican City

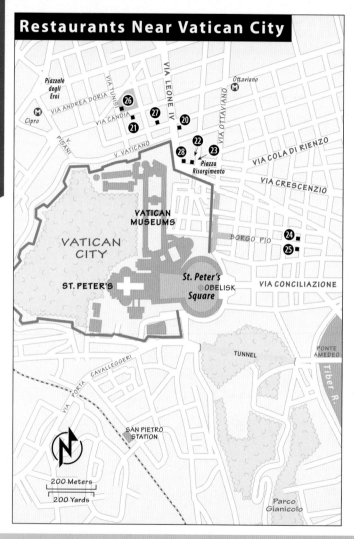

Piazzale degli Eroi

VIA TUNISI

VIA LEONE IV

VIA ANDREA DORIA

Ottaviano

Cipro

VIA CANDIA

VIA OTTAVIANO

26

27

20

21

V. PISANI

V. VATICANO

22

28

23

Piazza Risorgimento

VIA COLA DI RIENZO

VIA CRESCENZIO

VATICAN MUSEUMS

VATICAN CITY

BORGO PIO

24

25

ST. PETER'S

St. Peter's Square

OBELISK

VIA CONCILIAZIONE

PONTE AMEDEO

TUNNEL

Tiber R.

VIA PORTA CAVALLEGGERI

SAN PIETRO STATION

N

200 Meters

200 Yards

Parco Gianicolo

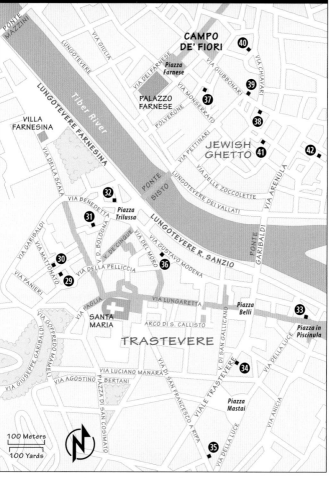

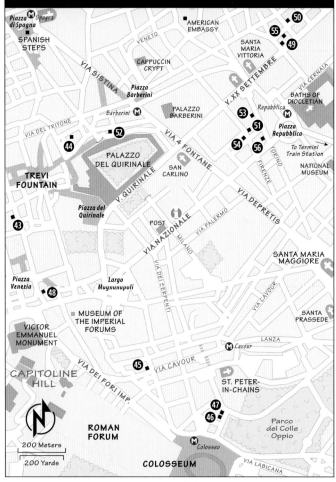

Restaurants near Trevi Fountain, Ancient Rome & Termini

Piazza di Spagna

SPANISH STEPS

VIA SISTINA

VENETO

AMERICAN EMBASSY

CAPPUCCIN CRYPT

SANTA MARIA VITTORIA

50
55
49

Piazza Barberini

VIA DEL TRITONE

Barberini

VIA XX SETTEMBRE

BATHS OF DIOCLETIAN

VIA CERNAIA

PALAZZO BARBERINI

Repubblica

Piazza Repubblica

53
52
51

VIA 4 FONTANE

44

PALAZZO DEL QUIRINALE

SAN CARLINO

V. QUIRINALE

54
56

TORINO

FIRENZE

To Termini Train Station

NATIONAL MUSEUM

TREVI FOUNTAIN

Piazza del Quirinale

POST

VIA NAZIONALE

VIA DEPRETIS

VIA PALERMO

MILANO

SANTA MARIA MAGGIORE

43

Piazza Venezia

48

Largo Magnanapoli

VIA DEI SERPENTI

SANTA PRASSEDE

MUSEUM OF THE IMPERIAL FORUMS

VIA CAVOUR

LANZA

VICTOR EMMANUEL MONUMENT

CAPITOLINE HILL

VIA DEI FORI IMP.

45

VIA CAVOUR

Cavour

ST. PETER-IN-CHAINS

47
46

Parco del Colle Oppio

N

200 Meters

200 Yards

ROMAN FORUM

Colosseo

COLOSSEUM

VIA LABICANA

Practicalities

Planning 184
Money. 185
Arrival in Rome 185
Helpful Hints 187
Getting Around Rome. 189
Staying Connected 193
Sightseeing Tips 195
Theft and Emergencies. 196
Activities 197
Resources from Rick Steves. 200
Italian Survival Phrases 201

PLANNING

Rome's best travel months—also the busiest and most expensive for flights and hotels—are May, June, September, and October. These months combine the convenience of peak season with pleasant weather. The summer heat in July and August can be brutal. In winter, Rome is cold and crisp (with rain a few days a week), there are fewer crowds, and some sights have shorter hours.

Make sure your passport is up to date (to renew, see www.travel.state.gov). Call your debit- and credit-card companies about your plans. Book hotel rooms well in advance, especially for peak season (May-Sept) and holidays. Consider buying travel insurance. Consider reservations for the Borghese Gallery (required) and the Colosseum and Vatican Museums (recommended). If you're traveling beyond Rome, research railpasses, train reservations, and car rentals.

Helpful Websites

Rome Tourist Information: www.turismoroma.it
Italian Tourist Information: www.italia.it
Passports and Red Tape: www.travel.state.gov
Cheap Flights: www.kayak.com (for international flights), www.skyscanner.net (for flights within Europe)
Airplane Carry-on Restrictions: www.tsa.gov
The Vatican: www.vaticanstate.va and www.museivaticani.va
Rome Entertainment and Current Events: www.inromenow.com
European Train Schedules: www.bahn.com
General Travel Tips: www.ricksteves.com (helpful info on train travel, rail passes, car rental, travel insurance, packing lists, and much more—plus updates to this book)

MONEY

Italy uses the euro currency: 1 euro (€1) = about $1.20. To convert euros to dollars add about 20 percent: €20 = about $24, €50 = about $60. (Check www.oanda.com for the latest exchange rates.)

Withdraw money from an ATM (often called a bancomat in Italy) using a debit card, just like at home. Visa and MasterCard are commonly used throughout Europe. Before departing, call your bank or credit-card company: Ask about international transaction fees, and alert them that you'll be making withdrawals in Europe. Many travelers bring a second debit/credit card as a backup. Small Roman businesses prefer cash, and some won't take credit cards at all, so withdraw large amounts (€250-300) from the ATM.

While American credit cards are accepted almost everywhere in Europe, even newer chip-style cards may not work in some payment machines (e.g., ticket kiosks). Be prepared to pay with cash, find a nearby cashier, or try entering your credit card's PIN (though you'll need to get the PIN from your bank before your trip).

To keep your cash and valuables safe, wear a money belt. But if you do lose your credit or debit card, report the loss immediately with a phone call: Visa (tel. 303/967-1096), MasterCard (tel. 636/722-7111), and American Express (tel. 336/393-1111).

ARRIVAL IN ROME

Fiumicino (Leonardo da Vinci) Airport

Rome's main airport has ATMs, banks, shops, bars, and a tourist information office (in Terminal 3, daily 9:00-17:30). For airport information, call 06-65951 or visit www.adr.it (airport code: FCO).

To get between the airport and downtown Rome, you have several options:

"Leonardo Express" Train: A direct train connects the airport and Rome's central Termini train station in 32 minutes for €14. Departures are twice hourly from roughly 6:00 to 23:00. From the airport's arrival gate, it's a 10-minute walk to the train, easily doable with wheeled luggage in tow. Follow signs to *Stazione/Railway Station.* Buy your ticket from a Trenitalia machine, the ticket office (biglietteria), or a newsstand, and then validate it in a green or yellow machine near the track. Make sure the train you board is going to the central "Roma Termini" station, as trains from the airport serve other destinations too.

Going from Termini to the airport, trains depart from track 24. Buy the €14 ticket at the platform from self-service machines or a newsstand.

Taxi: A taxi between Fiumicino and any destination in downtown Rome takes 45 minutes in normal traffic and costs an official fixed rate of €48, for up to four people with bags. To get the €48 fare, catch your taxi at the airport's taxi stand, and only use an official Rome city cab (white with the maroon *Roma Capitale* logo). Avoid unmarked, unmetered taxis or other cab companies; these guys will try to tempt you away from the taxi-stand lineup by offering an immediate (rip-off) ride. When you're departing Rome, your hotel can arrange a €48 taxi to the airport at any hour.

Rome Airport Shuttle Bus: These shared shuttle van services work best from your hotel to the airport, since it requires making a reservation (€25/1 person, extra people-€6 each, tel. 06-4201-4507 or 06-4201-3469, www.airportshuttle.it).

A useful video on the options for getting into the city from the airport is at www.romewalks.com.

Arrival at Ciampino Airport: Rome's smaller airport (tel. 06-6595-9515) handles charter flights and some budget airlines (including most Ryanair flights). To get to downtown Rome, the Terravision Express Shuttle bus connects Ciampino and Termini (about €5 and 2/hour, 45 minutes, www.terravision.eu). Rome Airport Shuttle (listed above) also offers service. A taxi should cost about €30.

Termini Train Station

Of Rome's four train stations, by far the most important is the centrally located Termini Station, which has connections to the airport.

Termini is a buffet of tourist services: information desks, cheap eateries, a large Sapori & Dintori supermarket (downstairs), late-hours banks, a good-sized bookstore, and 24-hour thievery—avoid anybody selling anything unless they're in a legitimate shop at the station.

Along track 24, about 100 yards down, you'll find the tourist information office (TI, daily 8:00-18:45), a post office, car rental desks, and baggage storage (€5/5 hours). The "Leonardo Express" train to Fiumicino (Leonardo da Vinci) Airport also runs from track 24.

Termini is a major transportation hub. The city's two Metro lines (A and B) intersect at Termini Metro station (downstairs). City buses, taxis, and the hop-on, hop-off bus tours leave from the front of the station.

To buy train tickets or make reservations, avoid Termini's long lines by buying from the station's ticket machines or from an uncrowded travel agency near your Rome hotel.

Other Arrival Points

Tiburtina Station: Some high-speed trains and many regional buses (e.g., from Siena or Sorrento) arrive here in the city's northeast corner (Metro: Tiburtina).

Arrival by Car: Don't drive in traffic-choked Rome. If you must arrive by car, get parking advice from your hotel. Or take the Settebagni exit, follow Centro signs, and park at the Villa Borghese underground garage (€18/day) near Metro: Spagna.

By Cruise Ship: Cruise ships dock at Civitavecchia (45 miles northwest of Rome), a 1.5-hour drive or 1-hour train ride to Rome. The easiest way to reach Rome is your cruise line's offered excursion. The cheapest option is by train: Catch the free shuttle bus from your ship to the port gate, then walk (about 25 minutes) or ride an orange city bus (€2, 3/hour) to Civitavecchia train station, where trains depart every 20 minutes to Rome's San Pietro, Termini, and other train stations (€10-15 round-trip). A taxi to central Rome (they'll be waiting at the dock, eager to overcharge you) should cost around €130 one-way.

HELPFUL HINTS

Tourist Information (TI): Rome has major tourist information offices (TIs) at Fiumicino Airport (Terminal 3, daily 9:00-17:30, longer in summer) and Termini train station (open until 18:45, exit by track 24 and walk 100 yards down along Via Giovanni Giolitti). Smaller kiosks—generally open daily 9:30-19:00—are located on Via Nazionale, near Piazza Navona, and near the Trevi Fountain. At any TI, get the freebies: a city map (also available from most hotels), and a listing of sights and hours. All share a website, www.turismoroma.it, but a better site for practical information is www.060608.it.

Other Travel Information: Rome's single best source of up-to-date tourist information is its call center, tel. 06-0608 (open daily 9:00-21:00, press 2 for English). For travel and English-language books, try Borri

Tipping

Tipping in Italy isn't as automatic and generous as it is in the US. At Italian restaurants that have waitstaff, a 10-15 percent "service" charge (servizio) is usually included in your bill's grand total. Italians don't tip beyond this, but if the service is exceptional, you can round up the bill by a euro or two. At hotels, it's polite to give porters a euro for each bag (another reason to pack light). To tip a taxi driver, round up to the nearest euro (for a €5.50 fare, give €6), or up to 10 percent for longer rides.

Books at Termini train station, or Feltrinelli International just off Piazza della Repubblica at Via Vittorio Emanuele Orlando 86. Other helpful English-oriented websites are www.inromenow.com, www.wantedinrome.com, and www.rome.angloinfo.com.

Hurdling the Language Barrier: Most people in the tourist industry—and virtually all young people—speak at least a little English. Still, learn the pleasantries like *buon giorno* (good day), *mi scusi* (pardon me), *per favore* (please), *grazie* (thank you), and *arrivederci* (goodbye). For more Italian survival phrases, ✪ see page 201.

Time: Italy's time zone is six/nine hours ahead of the east/west coasts of the US.

Business Hours: Most businesses are open Monday through Saturday, generally 10:00-19:00. Some small businesses and many banks close for lunch (roughly 13:00-15:30).

Holidays: Besides major holidays, Rome celebrates local festivals that can strike without warning, shutting down sights and bringing unexpected crowds. Verify dates at www.turismoroma.it or www.ricksteves.com/festivals.

Watt's Up? Europe's electrical system is 220 volts, instead of North America's 110 volts. You'll need an adapter plug with two round prongs, sold inexpensively at travel stores in the US. Most newer electronics (such as laptops, hair dryers, and battery chargers) convert automatically, so you won't need a separate converter.

Numbers and Stumblers: What Americans call the second floor of a building is the first floor in Europe. Europeans write dates as day/month/year. Commas are decimal points and vice versa—a dollar and half is 1,50, and there are 5.280 feet in a mile. Italy uses the metric system: A kilogram is 2.2 pounds; 1 liter is about a quart; and a kilometer is six-tenths of a mile. Temperature is measured in Celsius: 0°C = 32°F. For a rough conversion from Celsius to Fahrenheit, double the number and add 30.

Laundry: Your hotelier can direct you to the nearest self-serve launderette. Ondablu has a branch near Termini Station at Via Principe Amedeo 70b (about €8 to wash and dry a load, daily 8:00-21:00).

Pedestrian Safety: Use caution crossing Rome's chaotic streets. Follow locals like a shadow when you cross. Don't be a deer in the headlights, especially with oncoming scooters. Find a gap in the traffic and walk with confidence while making eye contact with approaching drivers. They won't hit you if they can tell where you intend to go.

Surviving Rome: The siesta is a key to survival in summertime Rome—try to schedule in a midday break at your air-conditioned hotel. WCs are scarce. Use them when you can, in any café or museum you patronize. Carry a water bottle to refill at Rome's numerous public drinking fountains.

GETTING AROUND ROME

While Rome's individual neighborhoods are walkable, to get across town you'll need to take buses, the Metro, and taxis. Consider it part of the Roman experience. For information, visit www.atac.roma.it, call 06-57003, or watch the helpful video "Understanding Rome's Public Transport" on YouTube.

Buying Tickets

All public transportation uses the same ticket. A single ticket costs €1.50 and is valid for one Metro ride (including transfers underground) plus unlimited city buses during a 100-minute period. Transit passes are sold in increments of 24 hours (€7), 48 hours (€12.50), 72 hours (€18), or one week (€24, about the cost of three taxi rides). The Roma Pass includes unlimited use of public transit but it's usually a poor value.

You can buy tickets and passes at some newsstands, tobacco shops (*tabacchi,* marked by a black-and-white T sign), and from machines at Metro stations and a few major bus stops (cash only), but not onboard. It's

Rome's Metro

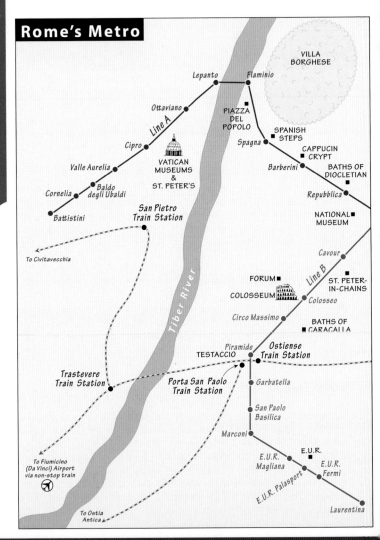

VILLA BORGHESE

Lepanto

Flaminio

Ottaviano

PIAZZA DEL POPOLO

Line A

SPANISH STEPS

Cipro

Spagna

CAPPUCIN CRYPT

VATICAN MUSEUMS & ST. PETER'S

Valle Aurelia

Barberini

BATHS OF DIOCLETIAN

Cornelia

Baldo degli Ubaldi

Repubblica

Battistini

San Pietro Train Station

NATIONAL MUSEUM

To Civitavecchia

Cavour

FORUM

Line B

ST. PETER-IN-CHAINS

Tiber River

COLOSSEUM

Colosseo

Circo Massimo

BATHS OF CARACALLA

Piramide

TESTACCIO

Ostiense Train Station

Trastevere Train Station

Porta San Paolo Train Station

Garbatella

San Paolo Basilica

To Fiumicino (Da Vinci) Airport via non-stop train

Marconi

E.U.R.

E.U.R. Magliana

E.U.R. Fermi

E.U.R. Palasport

To Ostia Antica

Laurentina

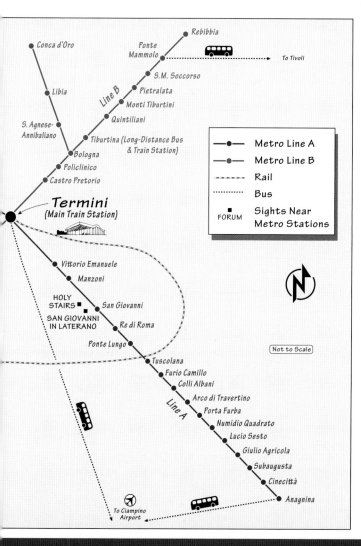

Conca d'Oro

Libia

S. Agnese-
Annibaliano

Line B

Quintiliani

Monti Tiburtini

Pietralata

S.M. Soccorso

Ponte
Mammolo

Rebibbia

To Tivoli

Tiburtina (Long-Distance Bus
& Train Station)

Bologna

Policlinico

Castro Pretorio

Termini
(Main Train Station)

	Metro Line A
	Metro Line B
	Rail
	Bus
FORUM	Sights Near Metro Stations

Vittorio Emanuele

Manzoni

HOLY
STAIRS

SAN GIOVANNI
IN LATERANO

San Giovanni

Re di Roma

Ponte Lungo

Tuscolana

Furio Camillo

Colli Albani

Arco di Travertino

Line A

Porta Furba

Numidio Quadrato

Lucio Sesto

Giulio Agricola

Subaugusta

Cinecittà

Anagnina

To Ciampino
Airport

Not to Scale

smart to stock up on tickets early in your visit rather than hunt around for an open vendor when you really need one.

By Metro

The Roman subway system (Metropolitana, or "Metro") is simple, with two lines you need to know—A and B—that intersect at Termini train station (line C is of little use to tourists). The Metro runs from 5:30 to 23:30 (Fri-Sat until 1:30 in the morning). Beware of pickpockets in crowded trains.

Validate your ticket by sticking it in the Metro turnstile (magnetic strip-side up, arrow-side first), and retrieving it. Watch others and imitate. To get through a Metro turnstile with a transit pass, use it just like a ticket.

By City Bus

Rome's buses are crowded-but-efficient people movers, and work like public buses anywhere. Every route has a number, each bus stop has a name, and every bus is headed to one end-of-the-line stop or the other. At any bus stop, read the posted sign with the list of stops (e.g. "Colosseo" or "Piazza Venezia") and figure out if that bus will take you where you want to go. For a good route planner in English, see www.atac.roma.it.

As you board, stamp your ticket in the box (magnetic strip-side down, arrow-side first), and retrieve it. Transit passes or the Roma Pass only need to be validated once, on your first trip. Watch out for pickpockets.

Two bus routes are especially helpful. Bus #64 cuts across the city, linking Termini train station to the Vatican, stopping at Piazza della Repubblica (near several sights), Via Nazionale (recommended hotels), Piazza Venezia (near Forum), Largo Argentina (near Pantheon and Campo de' Fiori), St. Peter's Basilica (get off just past the tunnel), and San Pietro Station. It's always jammed with tourists and pickpockets. Bus #40 is an express bus that mostly follows the #64 route (but ends at Castel Sant'Angelo), with fewer stops and crowds.

By Taxi

I use taxis in Rome more often than in other cities. They're reasonable and efficient in this big, hot metropolis. Three or four companions with more money than time should taxi almost everywhere. Besides, careening through Roman traffic in a speeding taxi is a video-game experience you won't soon forget.

Taxis start at €3, then charge about €1.50 per kilometer. Legitimate surcharges are clearly posted in the cab: €1.50 extra on Sun, €3.50 after 22:00, one suitcase rides free, and so on. Some sample fares: Termini train station to Vatican-€15; Termini to Colosseum-€7; Colosseum to Trastevere-€12; or look up your route at www.worldtaximeter.com. To tip, round up to the next euro, or (for longer rides) about 10 percent.

It's tough to wave down a taxi in Rome, especially at night. Find the nearest taxi stand (fermata dei taxi), have your hotel or restaurant call a taxi for you, or call them yourself (06-3570, 06-4994, or 06-6645). The meter starts when the call is received, generally adding a euro or two to the bill.

Beware of corrupt taxis. Make sure the meter is running and has been reset to around €3 (or around €5 if you've phoned for the taxi). If the meter is "broken," tell the driver to stop and let you out. Have a rough idea of what the ride should cost. Only use official taxis. They're white, with a taxi sign on the roof and a maroon logo on the door that reads *Roma Capitale*. If you think you've been overcharged, point to the price chart and ask the cabbie to explain it to you. Making a show of writing down the taxi number (to file a complaint) can motivate a driver to quickly settle the matter.

By Bike

Roman traffic is too stressful to use a bicycle as your main transportation. But joyrides are nice on small streets. There's a bike path along the west bank of the Tiber River, stretching from Ponte Regina Margherita (near Piazza del Popolo) to Ponte Sublicio.

Top Bike Rental rents bikes (€15/day), offers four-hour bike tours (€45 and up), and gives good tips on where to ride (located south of Termini station, at Via dei Quattro Cantoni 40, tel. 06-488-2893, www.topbikerental. com). Cool Rent, next to the Colosseo Metro stop, is cheaper (€10/day) but less helpful.

STAYING CONNECTED

Telephones

Making Calls: To call Italy from the US or Canada: Dial 011 (our international access code), then 39 (Italy's country code) and the local number. To call Italy from a European country: Dial 00 (Europe's international access code), then 39 and the local number. To call within Italy, just dial the local number. To call from Italy to another country: Dial 00 followed by the

Useful Phone Numbers

Police (English-speaking help): Tel. 113
Ambulance: Tel. 118
Directory Assistance (in English): Tel. 170
US Embassy: 24-hour emergency line—tel. 06-46741, non-emergency—tel. 06-4674-2420 (passport services Mon-Fri 8:30-12:30, closed Sat-Sun, Via Vittorio Veneto 121, http://it.usembassy.gov)
Canadian Embassy: Tel. 06-854-442-911 (Via Zara 30, www.italy.gc.ca)

country code (for example, 1 for the US or Canada), then the area code and number. If you're calling European countries whose phone numbers begin with 0, you'll usually have to omit that 0 when you dial. If you're calling from Italy (or elsewhere in Europe) using your US mobile phone, you may need to dial as if you're calling from the US.

Mobile Phones and Smartphones: Many US mobile phones work in Europe. Expect to pay around $1.70 a minute for phone calls and 50 cents per text message (somewhat less if you sign up for an international calling plan with your service provider). It's easy to buy a phone in Europe, which costs more up front but is cheaper by the call. You'll find mobile-phone stores selling cheap phones (for as little as $40 plus minutes) and SIM cards, at Fiumicino airport, Termini train station, and throughout Rome.

Smartphones give you access to the Internet and travel-oriented apps—helpful for planning your sightseeing, emailing hotels, and staying in touch. You can make free or cheap phone calls using Skype (www.skype.com), Google Talk (www.google.com/talk), or FaceTime (preloaded on many Apple devices). City Maps 2Go ($2, available from iTunes) gives you good searchable maps even when you're not online.

To avoid sky-high fees for data roaming, disable data roaming entirely, and only go online when you have free Wi-Fi (e.g., in a café or at your hotel). Or you could sign up for a global calling plan that cuts the per-minute cost of phone calls and texts, and a flat-fee data plan. Your normal plan may already include international coverage (T-Mobile's does).

For more information, talk to your service provider or see www.ricksteves.com/phoning.

Internet Access and Wi-Fi

Most hotels offer some form of free or cheap Internet access—either a shared computer in the lobby or Wi-Fi in the room. Otherwise, your hotelier can point you to the nearest Internet café, but be aware that Wi-Fi hotspots are not as plentiful in Rome as in many other large cities.

SIGHTSEEING TIPS

Hours: Hours of sights can change unexpectedly, so confirm the latest times at www.turismoroma.it, tel. 06-0608, or at a TI. Many sights stop admitting people 30-60 minutes before closing time, and guards start shooing people out before the actual closing time.

What to Expect: Important sights such as the Colosseum have metal detectors or conduct bag searches that will slow your entry. Others require you to check (for free) daypacks and coats. To avoid checking a small backpack, carry it under your arm like a purse as you enter.

Photos and videos are normally allowed, but flashes, tripods, and selfie sticks usually are not. Many sights only accept cash, no credit cards. Many offer guided tours and rent audioguides (€4-7). Expect changes—artwork can be in restoration, displayed elsewhere, or on tour. Most sights have an on-site café.

Churches: Many churches have divine art and free entry. They're generally open 7:30-12:00 and 15:00-19:00. Churches encourage a modest dress code (no shorts, bare shoulders, or miniskirts), and a few major churches enforce it. Bring coins to illuminate art in dim churches.

Discounts: Italy's national museums generally offer free admission to children under 18. Other museums may offer reduced admission for children and students (with International Student Identity Cards, www.isic.org). Senior discounts are generally only for EU residents (but it's worth asking). The Roma Pass is not worth the trouble.

Museum Reservations: They're required at the Borghese Gallery and recommended at the always-crowded Vatican Museums and Colosseum.

🎧 **Free Rick Steves Audio Tours:** I've produced free audio tours of many of Rome's best sights. With a mobile device, you can take me along as you tour the Colosseum, Roman Forum, Pantheon, St. Peter's Basilica, Vatican Museums, Sistine Chapel, Trastevere, Jewish Ghetto, and

Ostia Antica. You can download Rick Steves Audio Europe via Apple's App Store, Google Play, or the Amazon Appstore.

THEFT AND EMERGENCIES

Theft: While violent crime is rare in the city center, petty theft is rampant. With sweet-talking con artists meeting you at the station, well-dressed pickpockets on buses, and fast-fingered moms with babies at the ancient sites, Rome is a gauntlet of rip-offs.

The key is to keep alert to the possibility of theft, even when you're absorbed in the wonder, newness, and chaos of Rome. Don't trust kind strangers. Count your change carefully. Keep nothing important in your pockets. Assume beggars are pickpockets, and any commotion is simply a distraction by a team of thieves. Be on guard when crowds press together, especially while boarding and leaving buses and subways. I keep my valuables—passport, credit cards, crucial documents, and large amounts of cash—in a money belt that I tuck under my beltline.

Dial 113 for English-speaking police help. Report lost or stolen items to the police at Termini train station (tracks 11 or 20) or at Piazza Venezia. To replace a passport, file the police report, and then call your embassy to make an appointment (US embassy: tel. 06-46741, http://italy.usembassy. gov).

Medical Help: Dial 118 to summon an ambulance, or ask your ho telier for help. Anyone is entitled to free emergency treatment at public hospitals (Policlinico Umberto 1 is near Termini at Metro: Policlinico). For minor ailments, first visit a pharmacy (marked by a green cross), where qualified technicians routinely diagnose and prescribe. Embassies and hotels can recommend English-speaking doctors. MEDline has English-speaking doctors who make house calls to your hotel for about €150 (tel. 06-808-0995, www.soccorso-medico.com).

Practicalities

ACTIVITIES

Shopping

Most shops are open Monday to Saturday from roughly 9:00 to 13:00 and from 15:30 or 16:00 to 19:00 or 19:30. For everyday items, there's a full array at Termini train station, or try a department store (described below).

Shopping Neighborhoods: The Spanish Steps is the neighborhood for high-fashion boutiques, especially Via Condotti and Via Borgognona for the big-name shops. Via del Babuino is known for upscale international shops, and Via Margutta has designer boutiques, classy antiques, and art galleries. Via del Corso is a good, midrange shopping area.

Around Piazza Navona and Campo de' Fiori you'll find antiques, especially along Via de Coronari (between Piazza Navona and the river), Via Giulia (between Campo de' Fiori and the river), and Via Giubbonari (funkier items, near Campo de' Fiori).

If all you need are souvenirs, a surgical strike at any gift shop will do. Otherwise, stop at a department store, scout near the Vatican or in the Jewish Ghetto for religious items, hit the flea market and produce markets, or—if you're in a pinch—pick up some mementos at the airport on your way out of town.

Department Stores: The shopping complex under Termini train station is a convenient place to peruse clothes, bags, shoes, and perfume at several major Italian chain stores (most open daily 8:00-22:00).

A good upscale department store is La Rinascente (Via del Tritone 61). Besides deluxe brands, it has a fine design section with great and often affordable ideas for gifts, a magnificent rooftop terrace for a romantic *aperitivo,* good restaurants, free bathrooms, and a section of an ancient aqueduct in the basement (worth a quick visit). You'll find another branch on Piazza Fiume (east of the Borghese Gallery).

The Galleria Alberto Sordi is an elegant 19th-century "mall" (across from Piazza Colonna). UPIM is a popular midrange department store (many branches, including inside Termini train station, Via Nazionale 111, and Piazza Santa Maria Maggiore). Oviesse/OVS, a cheap clothing outlet, is near the Vatican Museums (on the corner of Via Candia and Via Mocenigo, Metro: Cipro) and also near Piazza Barberini (Via del Tritone 172, Metro: Barberini).

Practicalities

Flea Markets: The granddaddy of open-air street markets is the Porta Portese *mercato delle pulci* (flea market). This Sunday-morning market (6:30-13:00) is long and spindly. Start at Porta Portese (a gate in the old town wall) and stroll to the Trastevere train station, through a tacky parade of second-hand junk, cheap bras and shoes, con artists with shell games, pickpockets, food vendors, a few antique treasures, and priceless people-watching. (Catch bus #75 from Termini Station or tram #8 from Piazza Venezia to Viale Trastevere, and walk toward the noise.)

Open-Air Produce Markets: Rome's outdoor markets are museums for people-watchers. Many neighborhoods open up one street or square every Monday through Saturday from 7:00-13:30.

Campo de' Fiori's market has become quite touristy, but it's still a fun scene. Also try Via della Pace (near Piazza Navona) and Piazza delle Coppelle (near the Pantheon). In the Vatican neighborhood, consider the huge Mercato Trionfale, three blocks north of the Vatican Museums at Via Andrea Doria. Near the Termini train station is the small market along Via Balbo and the large Mercato Esquilino (on Via Turati, Metro: Vittorio Emanuele). My favorite is the gritty Mercato di Testaccio, a hit with photographers (Piazza Testaccio, near Metro: Piramide).

Getting a VAT Refund: If you purchase more than €155 (about $170) worth of goods at a single store, you may be eligible to get a refund of the 22 percent Value-Added Tax (VAT). Have the store fill out the paperwork. At the airport, get it stamped by customs and processed by a VAT refund company (at Fiumicino, you'll find customs stations in all terminals and Global Blue VAT refund counters at Terminals 3 and 5). Get more details from your merchant or see www.ricksteves.com/vat.

Customs for American Shoppers: You are allowed to take home $800 worth of items per person duty-free, once every 31 days. You can also bring in a liter of alcohol duty-free. As for food, you can take home many processed and packaged foods (e.g., vacuum-packed cheeses, chocolate, olive oil) but no fresh produce or meats. Any liquid-containing foods must be packed in checked luggage, a potential recipe for disaster. To check customs rules and duty rates, visit www.help.cbp.gov.

Nightlife

The best after-dark activity is to do what the Romans do: enjoy a leisurely meal, then grab a gelato and stroll the streets, past floodlit squares and fountains. For romantic ambience, head for Piazza Navona, the Pantheon, Campo de' Fiori, Trevi Fountain, the Spanish Steps, Via del Corso, or Trastevere.

The entertainment guide *Evento* (free at TIs and hotels) lists concerts, operas, dance, and films. Or visit www.inromenow.com, www.wantedinrome.com, or www.rome.angloinfo.com.

Classical Concerts: The Teatro dell'Opera, near Termini, has an active schedule of opera and classical concerts (Via Firenze 72, tel. 06-4816-0255, www.operaroma.it). Also near Termini, St. Paul's Within the Walls Episcopal Church hosts classical, opera, and Sunday-night candlelit concerts, with tickets usually available day-of-show (Via Napoli 58 at corner of Via Nazionale, tel. 06-482-6296, www.stpaulsrome.it). Trendy Romans flock way north of downtown to make the scene at the ultramodern Rome Auditorium, a.k.a. Parco della Musica (from Metro: Flaminio, catch tram #2 to Apollodoro, at Via Vittorio Veneto 96, tel. 06-8024-1281, www.auditorium.com).

Jazz: The venerable Alexanderplatz club, in the Vatican neighborhood, has music most evenings around 21:45 (Via Ostia 9, Metro: Ottaviano, closed in summer, tel. 06-3972-1867, www.alexanderplatzjazzclub.it). Il Pentagrappolo, east of the Colosseum, is an intimate enoteca with music Sept-June, Thu-Sat around 22:00 (Via Celimontana 21, tel. 06-709-6301, www.ilpentagrappolo.com).

Nightclubs: For late-night club-hopping (after 21:00), travel to Monte Testaccio. The small hill has cool caves housing funky restaurants and trendy clubs. Take the Metro to Piramide and follow the noise.

Tours

Guided Tours: Hiring your own personal tour guide can be delightful but pricey (roughly €60/hour). Less expensive are group tours, offering three-hour guided walks for small groups, usually led by American expats, charging about €25-30 per person. Try www.contexttravel.com or www.enjoyrome.com.

Hop-On, Hop-Off Bus Tours: For an intro to Rome, ride through the city on an open-air bus past the main sights (Colosseum, Circus Maximus, St. Peter's, and so on) while you listen to mediocre recorded commentary. Hop on at any of the stops along the 90-minute loop (e.g., at

Termini or Piazza Venezia), pay as you board, ride awhile, hop off to sightsee, and then catch the next bus (30 minutes later) to carry on. Traffic jams can make the bus dreadfully slow.

Car and Minibus Tours: Autoservizi Monti Concezio, run by English-speaking Ezio, offers private cars or minibuses with driver/guides (car-€40/hour, minibus-€45/hour, 3-hour minimum, also offers transfers between cities, mobile 335-636-5907, www.tourservicemonti.it, info@tourservicemonti.it).

RESOURCES FROM RICK STEVES

This pocket guide is one of dozens of titles in my series of guidebooks on European travel. I also produce a public television series, *Rick Steves' Europe,* and a public radio show, *Travel with Rick Steves.* My website, www.ricksteves.com, offers a wealth of free travel information including videos and podcasts of my shows, audio tours of Europe's great sights, travel forums, guidebook updates, my travel blog, and my guide to European rail passes—plus an online travel store and information on our tours of Europe.

How Was Your Trip? If you'd like to share your tips, concerns, and discoveries after using this book, please fill out the survey at www.ricksteves.com/feedback. It helps us and fellow travelers. Thanks, and *buon viaggio!*

Italian Survival Phrases

English	Italian	Pronunciation
Good day.	**Buon giorno.**	bwohn JOR-noh
Mr. / Mrs.	**Signore / Signora**	seen-YOH-ray / seen-YOH-rah
Miss	**Signorina**	seen-yoh-REE-nah
Do you speak English?	**Parla inglese?**	PAR-lah een-GLEH-zay
Yes. / No.	**Sì. / No.**	see / noh
I (don't) understand.	**(Non) capisco.**	(nohn) kah-PEES-koh
Please.	**Per favore.**	pehr fah-VOH-ray
Thank you.	**Grazie.**	GRAHT-see-ay
You're welcome.	**Prego.**	PREH-go
I'm sorry.	**Mi dispiace.**	mee dee-spee-AH-chay
Excuse me.	**Mi scusi.**	mee SKOO-zee
(No) problem.	**(Non) c'è un problema.**	(nohn) cheh oon proh-BLEH-mah
Good.	**Va bene.**	vah BEH-nay
Goodbye.	**Arrivederci.**	ah-ree-veh-DEHR-chee
one / two	**uno / due**	OO-noh / DOO-ay
three / four	**tre / quattro**	tray / KWAH-troh
five / six	**cinque / sei**	CHEEN-kway / SEH-ee
seven / eight	**sette / otto**	SEH-tay / OH-toh
nine / ten	**nove / dieci**	NOH-vay / dee-AY-chee
How much is it?	**Quanto costa?**	KWAHN-toh KOH-stah
Is it free?	**È gratis?**	eh GRAH-tees
Is it included?	**È incluso?**	eh een-KLOO-zoh
Can you help me?	**Può aiutarmi?**	pwoh ah-yoo-TAR-mee
Where can I buy / find...?	**Dove posso comprare / trovare...?**	DOH-vay POH-soh kohm-PRAH-ray / troh-VAH-ray
I'd like / We'd like...	**Vorrei / Vorremmo...**	voh-REH-ee / voh-REH-moh
...a room.	**...una camera.**	OO-nah KAH-meh-rah
...a ticket to ___.	**...un biglietto per ___.**	oon beel-YEH-toh pehr ___
Is it possible?	**È possibile?**	eh poh-SEE-bee-lay
Where is...?	**Dov'è...?**	doh-VEH
...tourist information	**...informazioni per turisti**	een-for-maht-see-OH-nee pehr too-REE-stee
...a cash machine	**...un bancomat**	oon BAHN-koh-maht
...the toilet	**...la toilette**	lah twah-LEH-tay
men	**uomini / signori**	WOH-mee-nee / seen-YOH-ree
women	**donne / signore**	DOH-nay / seen-YOH-ray
left / right	**sinistra / destra**	see-NEE-strah / DEH-strah
straight	**sempre dritto**	SEHM-pray DREE-toh
When does this open / close?	**A che ora apre / chiude?**	ah kay OH-rah AH-pray / kee-OO-day
At what time?	**A che ora?**	ah kay OH-rah
Just a moment.	**Un momento.**	oon moh-MEHN-toh
now / soon / later	**adesso / presto / tardi**	ah-DEH-soh / PREH-stoh / TAR-dee
today / tomorrow	**oggi / domani**	OH-jee / doh-MAH-nee

Practicalities

In the Restaurant

English	Italian	Pronunciation
I'd like / We'd like...	Vorrei / Vorremmo...	voh-REH-ee / vor-REH-moh
...to reserve...	...prenotare...	preh-noh-TAH-ray
...a table for one / two.	...un tavolo per uno / due.	oon TAH-voh-loh pehr OO-noh / DOO-ay
Is this table free?	È libero questo tavolo?	eh LEE-beh-roh KWEH-stoh TAH-voh-loh
The menu (in English), please.	Il menù (in inglese), per favore.	eel may-NOO (een een-GLEH-zay) pehr fah-VOH-ray
breakfast	colazione	koh-laht-see-OH-nay
lunch	pranzo	PRAHNT-soh
dinner	cena	CHEH-nah
service (not) included	servizio (non) incluso	sehr-VEET-see-oh (nohn) een-KLOO-zoh
cover charge	pane e coperto	PAH-nay ay koh-PEHR-toh
to go	da portar via	dah por-TAR VEE-ah
menu (of the day)	menù (del giorno)	may-NOO (dehl JOR-noh)
specialty of the house	specialità della casa	speh-chah-lee-TAH DEH-lah KAH-zah
first course (pasta, soup)	primo piatto	PREE-moh pee-AH-toh
main course (meat, fish)	secondo piatto	seh-KOHN-doh pee-AH-toh
side dishes	contorni	kohn-TOR-nee
bread / cheese	pane / formaggio	PAH-nay / for-MAH-joh
sandwich	panino	pah-NEE-noh
soup / salad	zuppa / insalata	TSOO-pah / een-sah-LAH-tah
meat	carni	KAR-nee
chicken	pollo	POH-loh
fish	pesce	PEH-shay
seafood	frutti di mare	FROO-tee dee MAH-ray
dessert	dolce	DOHL-chay
tap water	acqua del rubinetto	AH-kwah dehl roo-bee-NEH-toh
mineral water	acqua minerale	AH-kwah mee-neh-RAH-lay
milk	latte	LAH-tay
(orange) juice	succo (d'arancia)	SOO-koh (dah-RAHN-chah)
coffee / tea	caffè / tè	kah-FEH / teh
wine	vino	VEE-noh
red / white	rosso / bianco	ROH-soh / bee-AHN-koh
glass / bottle	bicchiere / bottiglia	bee-kee-EH-ray / boh-TEEL-yah
beer	birra	BEE-rah
Cheers!	Cin cin!	cheen cheen
More. / Another.	Di più. / Un altro.	dee pew / oon AHL-troh
The same.	Lo stesso.	loh STEH-soh
The bill, please.	Il conto, per favore.	eel KOHN-toh pehr fah-VOH-ray
Do you accept credit cards?	Accettate carte di credito?	ah-cheh-TAH-tay KAR-tay dee KREH-dee-toh
tip	mancia	MAHN-chah
Delicious!	Delizioso!	day-leet-see-OH-zoh

For more user-friendly Italian phrases, check out *Rick Steves' Italian Phrase Book & Dictionary* or *Rick Steves' French, Italian, and German Phrase Book*.

INDEX

A

Accommodations: *See* Sleeping
Aeneas (Bernini): 113
Airports: 185–186
Air travel resources: 184
Altar of Peace (Ara Pacis): 11, 143–144
Ancient Rome: 6–7, 122–130; eating, 16, 177; history of, 15–16, 22, 31, 42; maps, 17, 123, 127, 182; modern amenities, 16; religion in, 35; sights, 122–130; sleeping near, 161, 166; walking tours: Colosseum, 13–26; Roman Forum, 27–42
Antiques, shopping for: 197, 198
Antoninus Pius, Temple of: 36–37
Apollo and Daphne (Bernini): 110–111
Apollo Belvedere: 59–60
Appian Way: 153–155
Ara di Cesare: 35–36
Ara Pacis: 11, 143–144
Arch of Constantine: 24
Arch of Septimius Severus: 40
Arch of Titus: 31–33
Arrival in Rome: 185–187
Art museums: Capitoline Museums, 10, 129; daily reminder, 9; Etruscan Museum, 142; Galleria Doria Pamphilj, 11, 137; Montemartini Museum, 157; Museum of Roman Civilization, 157; National Museum of Rome, 10, 137–140; passes, 196. *See also* Borghese Gallery; Vatican Museums
ATMs: 185
Audio Tours, Rick Steves: 195–196
Augustus: 24, 31, 36, 49, 137, 138, 143–144

B

Barcaccia Fountain: 52
Basilica Aemilia: 37
Basilica Maxentius: 33
Basilica of Constantine: 33
Basilica San Pietro: *See* St. Peter's Basilica
Baths of Caracalla: 155
Baths of Diocletian: 11, 139–140
Belvedere Torso: 62
Benedict XVI, Pope: 101
Bernini, Gian Lorenzo: biographical sketch, 112; Borghese Gallery, 109–113, 115–117; Four Rivers Fountain, 45, 48; St. Peter's Basilica, 95–97; St. Peter's Square, 84, 86, 87; *St. Teresa in Ecstasy,* 11, 140; tomb of, 149; Trevi Fountain, 50–51, 137
Biking: 193
Bocca della Verità: 125
"Bone Crypt" (Cappuccin Crypt): 11, 142–143
Borghese Gallery: 105–119, 140; maps, 107, 116; orientation, 10, 106–107; reservations, 106, 184; the tour, 108–119
Borri Books: 187–188
Boy Extracting a Thorn: 129
Budgeting: eating, 171–172; hotels, 163; Roma Pass, 196
Buses: 192; tickets, 189; to/from airport, 186; tours, 199–201
Business hours: 188
Byron, George Gordon, Lord: 52

C

Cabs: *See* Taxis
Caligula: 86; Palace of, 37–38

Campidoglio: 11, 128
Campo de' Fiori: 44–45, 134; map, 181; market, 44, 134, 198; shopping, 197; sleeping near, 161, 166–167
Canova, Antonio: 108–109
Capitoline Hill: 10, 126, 128; map, 127
Capitoline Museums: 10, 129
Capuchin Crypt: 11, 142–143
Caravaggio: 80, 114–115, 134–135, 137
Car travel: 187
Castel Sant'Angelo: 11, 145–147
Catacombs: 11, 154–155; of Priscilla, 11, 144–145; of San Callisto, 154–155; of San Sebastiano, 154–155
Cathedrals: See Churches and cathedrals
Catherine of Siena, Saint: 136
Cell (mobile) phones: 194
Cemeteries: See Catacombs; Protestant Cemetery
Churches and cathedrals: sightseeing tips, 195; Domine Quo Vadis Church, 154; Gesù Church, 135; St. Paul's Outside the Walls, 157; St. Peter-in-Chains, 11, 124–125; San Clemente, 150; San Giovanni in Laterano, 147–148; San Ignazio, 136; San Luigi dei Francesi, 134–135; Santa Maria degli Angeli, 11, 139–140; Santa Maria della Vittoria, 11, 140; Santa Maria in Aracoeli, 128; Santa Maria in Cosmedin, 125; Santa Maria in Trastevere, 151; Santa Maria Maggiore, 148–149; Santa Maria sopra Minerva, 136; Santa Prassede, 149–150. See also St. Peter's Basilica
Ciampino Airport: 186
Circus Maximus: 124

Civitavecchia: 187
Classical concerts: 199
Climate: 184
Coffee: 172
Colosseum: 13–26, 122; eating near, 177; legacy of, 26; map, 18; modern amenities, 16; orientation, 10, 14; sleeping near, 166; walking tour, 15–26
Column of Phocas: 41–42
Constantine: 22, 63, 84; Arch of, 24; Basilica of, 33
Constantine Room (Vatican Museums): 66–67
Correggio, Antonio da: 118
Corsia Agonale: 48
Creation of Adam (Michelangelo): 71, 74
Credit cards: 184, 185
Cuisine: 172. See also Eating
Curia (Senate House): 39
Currency and exchange: 185
Customs regulations: 198

D
Daily reminder: 9
Danaë (Correggio): 118
David (Bernini): 109–110
Da Vinci, Leonardo: 80
Deposition (Caravaggio): 80
Deposition (Raphael): 117–118
Diana the Hunter: 113
Dining: See Eating
Diocletian, Baths of: 11, 139–140
Discounts: See Money-saving tips
Discus Thrower: 138
Disputa, The (Raphael): 69
Domine Quo Vadis Church: 154
Dying Gaul: 129

E

Eating: 169–182; Borghese Gallery, 107; budget meals, 171–172; cuisine, 172; Italian restaurant phrases, 202; listings, 173–178; maps, 179–182; price code, 170; tipping, 188; Vatican Museums, 55

Egyptian art, in the Vatican Museums: 57–59

Egyptian obelisks: 49, 86, 136

Electricity: 188

E-mail: 195

Embassies: 194

Emergencies: 197

Emperor Antoninus, Temple of: 36–37

Entertainment: 199

Esquiline: 25

Etruscan Museum: 142

E.U.R.: 157–158

Euro currency: 185

F

Feltrinelli International: 188

Fiumicino (Leonardo da Vinci) Airport: 185–186

Flea markets: 198

Food: See Eating; Gelato; Markets

Foro Romano: See Roman Forum

Four Rivers Fountain: 45, 48

Fra Angelico: 136

Francis I, Pope: 98

G

Galleria del Sordi: 50

Galleria Doria Pamphilj: 11, 137

Galleria e Museo Borghese: See Borghese Gallery

Garden of Eden: Temptation and Expulsion (Michelangelo): 74–75

Gelato: 49–50, 172

Gesù Church: 135

Giolitti's: 49–50

Guidebooks, Rick Steves: 200

Guided tours: 199; Borghese Gallery, 106; Colosseum, 14; Roman Forum, 28; St. Peter's Basilica, 83; Vatican Museums, 54–55

H

Hadrian: 24, 48, 132, 145–147

Hadrian's Villa: 159–160

Heart of Rome walk: 43–52; map, 46–47

Helpful hints: 187–189

History: 22, 31, 42

Holidays: 188

Holy Stairs: 148

Hotels: See Sleeping

House of the Vestal Virgins: 38–39

I

Imperial Forums: 126

Internet access: 195

Italian restaurant phrases: 202

Italian survival phrases: 201

Itineraries: 8–9, 12

J

Jazz music: 199

Jewish Museum: 153

Jewish Quarter: 152–153

John Paul II, Pope: 101

John XXIII, Pope: 95

Julius Caesar: 27, 31, 39, 137–138; Temple of, 35–36

K

Keats, John: 156–157

L

Language: 188; restaurant phrases, 202; survival phrases, 201
Laocoön: 60–62
Largo Argentina: 44, 131
Largo 16 Ottobre 1943: 152
Last Judgment (Michelangelo): 76–77
Laundry: 189
Leonardo da Vinci Airport: 185–186
"Leonardo Express" Train: 185–186
Liberation of St. Peter (Raphael): 68

M

Map Gallery (Vatican Museums): 65
Markets: 172, 198; Campo de' Fiori, 44, 134, 198; Testaccio, 155–156, 198; Trionfale, 175, 198
Medical help: 197
Metric system: 188–189
Metro: 192; map, 190–191; tickets, 189
Michelangelo: 62, 70, 136; St. Peter-in-Chains Church, 11, 124–125; St. Peter's Basilica, 92–93, 95, 99–101; Santa Maria degli Angeli, 11, 139–140; Sistine Chapel, 70–78
Mobile phones: 194
Money: 185
Money belts: 185, 197
Money-saving tips: 195; eating, 171–172; hotels, 163; Roma Pass, 196
Montemartini Museum: 157
Monte Palatino: 10, 122–124
Monte Testaccio: 155–156, 156; night-clubs, 199
Moses (Michelangelo): 124

"Mouth of Truth": 125
Mummies, in the Vatican Museums: 58
Musei Capitolini: 10, 129
Musei Vaticani: *See* Vatican Museums
Museo Borghese: *See* Borghese Gallery
Museo dell'Ara Pacis: 11, 143–144
Museo della Via Ostiense: 156
Museo Ebraico: 153
Museo Nazionale Romano Palazzo Massimo alle Terme: 10, 137–140
Museum of Roman Civilization: 157
Museum of the Altar of Peace: 11, 143–144
Museum of the Imperial Forums: 126
Music: 199
Mussolini, Benito: 22, 126, 157

N

National Museum of Rome: 10, 137–140
Neighborhoods: 6–8; map, 7. *See also specific neighborhoods*
Nightclubs: 199
Nightlife: 199
North Rome: 7, 140–145; eating, 174; maps, 141, 179

O

Obelisks: *See* Egyptian obelisks
Opera: 199
Ostia Antica: 158–159

P

Palatine Hill: 10, 122–124
Palazzo Madama: 48
Palazzo Massimo alle Terme: 10, 137–140
Pantheon: 10, 48, 132–134
Pantheon neighborhood: 7, 131–137;

eating, 173–174; maps, 46–47, 131,
179; sights, 131–137; sleeping, 161,
167; walking tour, 43–52
Papal audiences: 83
Papal succession: 91
Parliament building: 49
Passports: 184
Pauline Bonaparte as Venus (Canova):
108–109
Pedestrian safety: 189
Peter, Saint: 93–95, 99, 147, 148, 154
Phone numbers, useful: 194
Phones: 193–194
Piazza Capranica: 49
Piazza Colonna: 50
Piazza del Campidoglio: 11, 128
Piazza del Popolo: 144
Piazza di Spagna: 51
Piazza Navona: 45, 48, 134; eating near,
173; map, 46–47; shopping, 197
Piazza Venezia: 126, 144; map, 127;
sleeping near, 165
Pietà (Michelangelo): 99–101
Pilgrim's Rome: 147–150; map, 149
Pinacoteca (Borghese Gallery): 115–119
Pinacoteca (Vatican Museums): 80
Planning tips: 8–9, 12, 184; itineraries,
8–9, 12
Police: 194
Pollaiuolo, Antonio: 102
Popes: seeing, 83; succession, 91. *See
also specific popes*
Porta Pinciana: 142
Porta Portese: 198
Porta San Paolo: 156
Portico d'Ottavia: 152–153
Priscilla, catacombs of: 11, 144–145
Protestant Cemetery: 156–157

Pyramid of Gaius Cestius: 156

R

Rape of Proserpine (Bernini): 111, 113
Raphael: 117–118, 134, 151–152;
Vatican Museums, 80; Villa Farnesina,
151–152
Raphael Rooms (Vatican Museums):
67–69; map, 67
Reader feedback: 200
Religion: in ancient Rome, 35. *See also*
Churches and cathedrals; Vatican City
Renaissance art, in the Vatican
Museums: 67–69
Restaurants: *See* Eating
Roman Forum: 27–42, 122; map, 29; ori-
entation, 10, 28; walking tour, 30–42
Roman Holiday (movie): 125
Romans, ancient: *See* Ancient Rome
Roma Pass: 196
Rome Airport Shuttle Bus: 186
Rome from the Sky: 11, 130
Rostrum (Rostri): 39–40
Round Room (Vatican Museums): 62–63

S

Sacred and Profane Love (Titian):
118–119
St. Agnes Church: 45, 48
St. Jerome (da Vinci): 80
St. Paul's Outside the Walls: 157
St. Peter-in-Chains Church: 11, 124–125
St. Peter's Basilica: 81–103, 145; climb-
ing the dome, 82, 102–103; map, 89;
orientation, 10, 82–83; walking tour,
87–103
St. Peter's Square: 84, 86–87; map, 85
St. Teresa in Ecstasy (Bernini): 11, 140

San Callisto, catacombs of: 154–155
San Clemente Church: 150
San Giovanni in Laterano Church: 147–148
San Ignazio Church: 136
San Luigi dei Francesi Church: 134–135
San Pietro in Vincoli: 11, 124–125
San Sebastiano, catacombs of: 154–155
Santa Maria degli Angeli: 11, 139–140
Santa Maria della Vittoria: 11, 140
Santa Maria in Aracoeli Church: 128
Santa Maria in Cosmedin Church: 125
Santa Maria in Trastevere Church: 151
Santa Maria Maggiore Church: 148–149
Santa Maria sopra Minerva Church: 136
Santa Prassede Church: 149–150
Scala Santa: 148
School of Athens (Raphael): 68–69
Seasons: 184
Self-guided tours: See Walking tours
Septimius Severus, Arch of: 40
Shelley, Percy: 156–157
Shopping: 197–198; hours, 188; neighborhoods, 197; VAT refunds, 198
Sights: 121–160; at a glance, 10–11; daily reminder, 9; general tips, 195–196; itineraries, 8–9, 12; passes, 196; quick tips, 12. See also Walking tours; and specific sights
"Sinking Boat" Barcaccia Fountain: 52
Sistine Chapel: 70–78; maps, 71, 73
Sleeping: 161–168; budget tips, 163; listings, 164–168; price code, 163; reservations, 162, 184; typical hotel room, 162
Smartphones: 194
South Rome: 153–157

Spanish Steps: 51–52, 143; eating near, 174; shopping, 197
Subway: See Metro
Symbols key: 8

T

Taxes: VAT refunds, 198
Taxis: 192–193; to/from airport, 186; tipping, 188
Tazza d'Oro Casa del Caffè: 49
Teatro dell'Opera: 199
Telephone numbers, useful: 194
Telephones: 193–194
Temple of Antoninus Pius and Faustina: 36–37
Temple of Castor and Pollux: 37–38
Temple of Julius Caesar: 35–36
Temple of Saturn: 41
Temple of Venus and Rome: 25–26
Temple of Vesta: 38
Terme di Caracalla: 155
Termini Train Station: 8, 186–187; eating near, 178; maps, 138, 182; sights near, 137–140; sleeping near, 161, 164–165
Testaccio: 8, 155–157; map, 156; market, 155–156, 198; nightclubs, 199
Theft alert: 196–197
Tiburtina Station: 187
Time zone: 188
Tipping: 188
Titian: 118–119, 137
Titus, Arch of: 31–33
Tivoli: 159–160
Toilets: 16
Tour guides: 199
Tourist information: 187–188; websites, 184

Tours: *See* Guided tours; Walking tours
Train station: *See* Termini Train Station
Train travel: 185–186
Trajan's Column: 10, 125–126
Trajan's Market: 10, 125–126
Transfiguration, The (Raphael): 80
Transportation: around Rome, 189–193;
    to Rome, 185–187
Trastevere: 8, 150–153; eating, 175–177;
    map, 181; sleeping, 161, 167
Travel insurance: 184
Treasury Museum (St. Peter's Basilica):
    102
Tre Scalini: 48
Trevi Fountain: 11, 50–51, 137; eating
    near, 177; map, eating, 182
Trionfale market: 175, 198

V

Vatican City: 7, 145–147; about, 102;
    eating near, 175; guided tours, 83;
    maps, 85, 146, 179; nightlife, 199; pa-
    pal audiences, 83; St. Peter's Square,
    84, 86–87; sights, 145–147; sleeping
    near, 161, 168; views of, 65. *See also*
    St. Peter's Basilica; Vatican Museums
Vatican Museums: 53–80, 145; eating,
    55; guided tours, 54–55; maps, 56,
    61, 63, 67; orientation, 10, 54–55;

Pinacoteca, 80; Sistine Chapel,
    70–78; the tour, 56–80
VAT refunds: 198
Vestal Virgins, House of the: 38–39
Via Appia: 153–155
Via Condotti: 52, 144, 197
Via Cuccagna: 45
Via de Crociferi: 50
Via del Babuino: 197
Via del Corso: 50, 144
Via del Portico d'Ottavia: 153
Via del Salvatore: 48
Via Sacra: 30–31, 33
Victor Emmanuel Monument: 11,
    129–130
Villa Adriana: *See* Hadrian's Villa
Villa Borghese Gardens: 140, 142
Villa d'Este: 159–160
Villa Farnesina: 151–152

W

Walking tours: Borghese Gallery,
    108–119; Colosseum, 15–26; heart of
    Rome, 43–52; Roman Forum, 27–42;
    St. Peter's Basilica, 87–103; Vatican
    Museums, 56–80
Weather: 184
Websites: 184
Wi-Fi: 195

Start your trip at

Our website enhances this book and turns

Explore Europe

At ricksteves.com you can browse through thousands of articles, videos, photos and radio interviews, plus find a wealth of money-saving travel tips for planning your dream trip. And with our mobile-friendly website, you can easily access all this great travel information anywhere you go.

TV Shows

Preview the places you'll visit by watching entire half-hour episodes of Rick Steves' Europe (choose from all 100 shows) on-demand, for free.

ricksteves.com

your travel dreams into affordable reality

Radio Interviews

Enjoy ready access to Rick's vast library of radio interviews covering  travel tips and cultural insights that relate specifically to your Europe travel plans.

Travel Forums

Learn, ask, share! Our online community of savvy travelers is a great resource for first-time travelers to Europe, as well as seasoned pros. You'll find forums on each country, plus travel tips and restaurant/hotel reviews. You can even ask one of our well-traveled staff to chime in with an opinion.

Travel News

Subscribe to our free Travel News e-newsletter, and get monthly updates from Rick on what's happening in Europe.

Audio Europe™

Pack Light and Right

Gear up for your next adventure at ricksteves.com

Light Luggage

Pack light and right with Rick Steves' affordable, custom-designed rolling carry-on bags, backpacks, day packs and shoulder bags.

Accessories

From packing cubes to moneybelts and beyond, Rick has personally selected the travel goodies that will help your trip go smoother.

Shop at ricksteves.com

Rick Steves has

Experience maximum Europe

Save time and energy

This guidebook is your independent-travel toolkit. But for all it delivers, it's still up to you to devote the time and energy it takes to manage the preparation and logistics that are essential for a happy trip. If that's a hassle, there's a solution.

Rick Steves Tours

A Rick Steves tour takes you to Europe's most interesting places with great guides and small groups

great tours, too!

with minimum stress

of 28 or less. We follow Rick's favorite itineraries, ride in comfy buses, stay in family-run hotels, and bring you intimately close to the Europe you've traveled so far to see. Most importantly, we take away the logistical headaches so you can focus on the fun.

Join the fun

This year we'll take thousands of free-spirited travelers—nearly half of them repeat customers—along with us on four dozen different itineraries, from Ireland to Italy to Istanbul. Is a Rick Steves tour the right fit for your travel dreams? Find out at ricksteves.com, where you can also request Rick's latest tour catalog.

Europe is best experienced with happy travel partners. We hope you can join us.

See our itineraries at ricksteves.com

A Guide for Every Trip

BEST OF GUIDES

Full-color guides in an easy-to-scan format, focusing on top sights and experiences in popular destinations

Best of England
Best of Europe
Best of France
Best of Germany

Best of Ireland
Best of Italy
Best of Scotland
Best of Spain

COMPREHENSIVE GUIDES

City, country, and regional guides printed on Bible-thin paper. Packed with detailed coverage for a multi-week trip exploring iconic sights and more

Amsterdam &
  the Netherlands
Barcelona
Belgium: Bruges, Brussels,
  Antwerp & Ghent
Berlin
Budapest
Croatia & Slovenia
Eastern Europe
England
Florence & Tuscany
France
Germany
Great Britain
Greece: Athens &
  the Peloponnese
Iceland

Ireland
Istanbul
Italy
London
Paris
Portugal
Prague & the Czech Republic
Provence & the French
  Riviera
Rome
Scandinavia
Scotland
Sicily
Spain
Switzerland
Venice
Vienna, Salzburg & Tirol

Rick Steves books are available from your favorite bookseller.
Many guides are available as ebooks.

POCKET GUIDES
Compact guides for shorter city trips

Amsterdam   Italy's Cinque Terre   Prague
Athens   London   Rome
Barcelona   Munich & Salzburg   Venice
Florence   Paris   Vienna

SNAPSHOT GUIDES
Focused single-destination coverage

Basque Country: Spain & France
Copenhagen & the Best of Denmark
Dublin
Dubrovnik
Edinburgh
Hill Towns of Central Italy
Krakow, Warsaw & Gdansk
Lisbon
Loire Valley
Madrid & Toledo
Milan & the Italian Lakes District
Naples & the Amalfi Coast
Nice & the French Riviera
Normandy
Northern Ireland
Norway
Reykjavik
Rothenburg & the Rhine
Sevilla, Granada & Southern Spain
St. Petersburg, Helsinki & Tallinn
Stockholm

CRUISE PORTS GUIDES
Reference for cruise ports of call

Mediterranean Cruise Ports
Scandinavian & Northern European
  Cruise Ports

TRAVEL SKILLS & CULTURE
Greater information and insight

Europe 101: History and Art for
  the Traveler
Europe Through the Back Door:
  the Travel Skills Handbook
European Christmas
European Easter
European Festivals
Postcards from Europe
Travel as a Political Act

PHRASE BOOKS & DICTIONARIES

French
French, Italian & German
German
Italian
Portuguese
Spanish

PLANNING MAPS

Britain, Ireland & London
Europe
France & Paris
Germany, Austria & Switzerland
Iceland
Ireland
Italy
Spain & Portugal

PHOTO CREDITS

Avalon Travel
An imprint of Perseus Books
A Hachette Book Group company
1700 Fourth Street
Berkeley, CA 94710, U.S.A.

Printed in China by RR Donnelley
Third Edition
Fifth printing October 2019

ISBN 978-1-63121-559-9
ISSN 2158-6152

For the latest on Rick's lectures, guidebooks, tours, public radio show, and public television series, contact Rick Steves' Europe, Inc., 130 Fourth Avenue North, Edmonds, WA 98020, tel. 425/771-8303, ricksteves.com, rick@ricksteves.com.

RICK STEVES' EUROPE
Managing Editor: Jennifer Madison Davis
Special Publications Manager: Risa Laib
Editors: Glenn Eriksen, Tom Griffin, Katherine Gustafson, Suzanne Kotz, Cathy Lu, John Pierce, Carrie Shepherd
Editorial & Production Assistant: Jessica Shaw
Researcher: Ian Watson
Graphic Content Director: Sandra Hundacker
Maps & Graphics: David C. Hoerlein, Lauren Mills, Mary Rostad

AVALON TRAVEL
Senior Editor and Series Manager: Madhu Prasher
Editor: Jamie Andrade
Associate Editor: Sierra Machado
Copy Editor: Kelly Lydick
Proofreader: Rebecca Freed
Indexer: Stephen Callahan
Production & Typesetting: McGuire Barber Design, Christine DeLorenzo
Cover Design: Kimberly Glyder Design
Interior Design: Darren Alessi
Cover Photos: Basilica St Peter and the Tiber River © Mapics | Dreamstime.com
Maps & Graphics: Kat Bennett, Mike Morgenfeld, Brice Ticen

ABOUT THE AUTHORS

Rick Steves

Since 1973, Rick has spent about four months a year exploring Europe. His mission: to empower Americans to have European trips that are fun, affordable, and culturally broadening. Rick produces a best-selling guidebook series, a public television series, and a public radio show, and organizes small-group tours that take over 20,000 travelers to Europe annually. He does all of this with the help of a hardworking, well-traveled staff of 100 at Rick Steves' Europe in Edmonds, Washington, near Seattle. When not on the road, Rick is active in his church and with advocacy groups focused on economic justice, drug policy reform, and ending hunger. To recharge, Rick plays piano, relaxes at his family cabin in the Cascade Mountains, and spends time with his partner Trish, son Andy, and daughter Jackie. Find out more about Rick at www.ricksteves.com and on Facebook.

Gene Openshaw

Gene has co-authored a dozen Rick Steves books, specializing in writing walks and tours of Europe's cities, museums, and cultural sights. He also contributes to Rick's public television series, produces tours for Rick Steves Audio Europe, and is a regular guest on Rick's public radio show. Outside of the travel world, Gene has co-authored *The Seattle Joke Book*. As a composer, Gene has written a full-length opera called *Matter* (soundtrack available on Amazon), a violin sonata, and dozens of songs. He lives near Seattle with his daughter, enjoys giving presentations on art and history, and roots for the Mariners in good times and bad.

FOLDOUT COLOR MAP

The foldout map on the opposite page includes:
- A map of Rome on one side
- Maps of South Rome, Rome Transportation, Colosseum, St. Peter's Basilica, Roman Forum, and Heart of Rome Walk on the other side